HAUNTED SHAWNEE, OKLAHOMA

HAUNTED SHAWNEE, OKLAHOMA

TANYA McCOY AND JEFF PROVINE

Published by Haunted America
A Division of The History Press
Charleston, SC
www.historypress.com

First published 2020

Manufactured in the United States

ISBN 9781467146869

Library of Congress Control Number: 2020938621

Notice: The information in this book is true and complete to the best of our knowledge. It is offered without guarantee on the part of the authors or The History Press. The authors and The History Press disclaim all liability in connection with the use of this book.

DEDICATIONS

I dedicate this book to my amazing paranormal team and support group: Chris Borthick, Keisha Pratt-Officer, Debra Breshears, Kim Selvey, Alonie McKown and Shelly and Jess Goodman. You guys are the best around, and a person could not ask for better. You give 110 percent. You are the hardest-working, most creative group I have ever had the pleasure of working with. I am so grateful for all you do.

As always, I also dedicate this work to my loving husband, Clinton Womack, and my family for their love and support.

And last but not least, I would like to dedicate this book to my best friend, teammate, supporter, confidant and soul sister, Whitney Wilson, who helps to keep me grounded when my spontaneous, crazy ideas send her head into a whirlwind. I love you dearly, and I could not do this without you.

—Tanya

To Courtney, for abiding late nights with the lights on.

—Jeff

CONTENTS

Contents

ACKNOWLEDGEMENTS

A special thanks goes out to the Pottawatomie County Historical Museum and the Tecumseh Historical Society, which have made all our research painless and have allowed us to use their amazing programs and resources. The work these organizations do for the community is amazing and greatly appreciated by all researchers.

A special thanks also goes to the businesses of Shawnee that were willing to share their stories and open their doors to us and the idea of sharing a few ghostly tales with the residents of Shawnee and Oklahoma. We would also like to thank St. Gregory's Abbey, Chief Kidney and the Tecumseh Police Department and writer Steven E. Wedel for taking the time to chat with us. We would also like to give our thanks to researchers Logan Corelli, Kale Epperson and Jim Whitehead for sharing their knowledge.

And Tanya would like to send a very special thank-you to her co-author, Jeff Provine, who had to put up with my crazy schedule and who was usually left waiting for me to do my "crunch-time" writing. You are an amazing co-author, and I appreciate everything you do to make our books turn out amazingly and on time.

Truly the Wild West

History of the Shawnee Area

The land that would become Shawnee, Oklahoma, rests at the heart of the Cross Timbers ecological region. There, the dense woodlands of the east begin to thin out and become the wide-open prairie of the Great Plains. Since time immemorial, these woods and grasslands have teemed with life, from sauntering black bears to herds of bison and endless species of birds, insects, reptiles and mammals. Native peoples have hunted on these lands for thousands of years. Evidence of their hunts, including loose arrowheads made from knapping flint, may still be found today. Even in those early days, this was a land of mystery and wilderness with secrets to hide.

European explorers eventually crisscrossed the land, always noting the hardness of the trees. Geologically, the Cross Timbers is a rugged terrain, with sandy soil derived from the sandstone, shale and limestone beneath. Sprawling thickets of post oak and blackjack oak stretched for miles, serving as a barrier between worlds, according to nineteenth-century explorer and trader Josiah Gregg. He stated in 1840 that the landscape varied "in width from five to thirty miles and entirely cut off the communication betwixt the interior prairies and those of the Great Plains." Captain Randolph B. Marcy noted in 1852 that the trees were pleasantly spaced to allow wagons through, which only came after years of traveling traders, like Gregg, carved out trails in the scrubby underbrush.

While accompanying the Ellison Expedition, famed author Washington Irving passed through today's Pottawatomie County in November 1832. A marker commemorating the adventure stands on the north side of Main

Street, near the Santa Fe Depot, in Shawnee's Centennial Park. On his return to the East, Irving wrote in *A Tour on the Prairie*, "I shall not easily forget the mortal toil, and the vexations of flesh and spirit, that we underwent occasionally, in our wanderings through the Cross Timber. It was like struggling through forests of cast iron."

Trailblazer Jesse Chisholm founded a trading post just east of today's Asher at what was called Chisholm Spring in 1847. It proved to be a useful point, especially since the West Shawnee Trail served as one of the early routes for cattle drives. While some cattlemen drove their longhorns east, toward Arkansas, others rounded the dense Cross Timbers by passing Chisholm Spring and going up what is today Kickapoo Avenue before turning northeast. The settlement and trail ended in 1862, when Chisholm left for Kansas after the Civil War had slashed the East's demand for beef. There was a brief rebirth of the trail after the war ended, but cattlemen soon preferred Chisholm's trail farther west, which had wider ranges for pasture and fewer settlers who proved to be a hassle.

The permanent settlement of the region began with the Indian Removal Acts of the 1830s, which set aside land as reservations for the Creeks and Seminoles, who had been displaced from their ancestral lands in the Southeast. Following the Civil War, the United States government constricted their tribal lands, crafting space for new reservations. The Sac and Fox tribes were the first to officially arrive after 1870; they had been moved from their settlements in Iowa, where they had already been pushed west from Illinois. The Absentee Shawnee, the members of the tribe who had refused to move to the reservation in Kansas and instead settled along the Canadian River, were met by incoming Citizen Potawatomi, who were themselves leaving Kansas as their lands faced further White encroachment. In 1883, the Iowa and Kickapoo from Mexico were relocated to the southwest portion of the Sac and Fox Reservation by executive order. Clashes broke out over what land belonged to whom, and finally, the federal government mapped borders that lasted until the land runs.

Along with the settlers came education. Quakers established a mission just south of what became Shawnee in 1871. In 1876, following the request of the Catholic members of the Citizen Potawatomi, Benedictine monks established the Sacred Heart Mission, which had boarding schools for boys and girls near Chisholm's old trading post. Father Thomas Bergh wrote in 1886, while visiting the mission, "It is good land, undulating and well-watered and, where cultivated, grows the usual European crops....There can be no doubt that the U.S. government will not be able much longer to restrain the covetousness of the Whites who hover all around the territory and only wait the chance to rush in."

The father's words were prophetic. Unassigned Lands Boomers had been storming into the nearby Unassigned Lands for six years. The Santa Fe Railroad came through the territory only months after Bergh's observation, and in 1889, the two million acres were opened with the first-ever land run. It did not take long for settlers to call for plots across the Indian Meridian, despite them being owned by the Potawatomi and Shawnee. Less than a year after the first run, on June 25, 1890, the federal government signed a new treaty that reduced the land that was directly settled by the tribes to allotments. The surplus land was claimed by runners in chaotic rushes that grew wilder with each race.

The first area opened was the 900,000-acre tract that was broken up into 160-acre homesteads. Twenty thousand would-be settlers sprinted for only six thousand sections, meaning that the vast majority of them were facing disappointment by the day's end. At noon on September 22, 1891, cannons were fired to begin the run. Many of the settlers were headed toward the soon-to-be county seat at Tecumseh, only to be halted at the edge of the townsite by soldiers. The plans had been changed for the location of the courthouse at the heart of town, so surveyors had to restart mapping the middle of town. Again, they had to wait. The next morning, ten thousand people lined up around Tecumseh. Many of them were chomping at the bit, as they had waited a whole day under the watchful eye of soldiers. Others hadn't had any luck the day before, so this was their second chance at a town lot. At noon, the soldiers fired rifles to unleash a bedlam that made even the previous runs look tame.

In the midst of it, the settlement of 1891 claimed its first victim: Doc Roundtree. There are several stories about what actually happened to him. Some say that his horse had jumped the gun before noon and that the soldiers shot him as a lesson to sooners. More likely is that Roundtree successfully made the run, leapt off his horse to stake his claim downtown and was then trampled to death by the horses behind him. Numerous others were injured, either in the run itself or in the fights that broke out over who claimed which site first. Fortson wrote in his *History of Pott County* that as many as six people would get into a brawl over one piece of land, although the presence of the military kept things "a well-regulated affair."

Even after the run was over, there was plenty of unlawful activity that took place. One swindler faked a claim in the alley south of the opera house and offered to sell it to anyone coming by. Once it was sold, the swindler disappeared, and the neighbors eventually let the proud new "owner" know that alleys could not be claimed. When the duped fellow left, the swindler wound his way back to the alley and repeated the con all over again.

While some tried to use their wits to obtain land, others used brute force for outright claim-jumping. Runner Charles J. Benson told Fortson the story of a neighbor who had built a log cabin on her claim and asked him to keep an eye on it while she made a trip. Not long after she had left, Benson noticed the door to her cabin was open. When he went to investigate, the claim-jumper inside knocked him out with a left-handed punch.

Order eventually settled in the new territory. It had been separated into County A in the north and County B in the south. A vote of 841 to 207 in November 1892 renamed County B Pottawatomie after the Potawatomi people who had already settled there. Courts opened and sorted out legally which claimant owned which lot. Another land run in 1895 added the panhandle of the county from Kickapoo land. This run was even more chaotic than the others, prompting the government to end the practice of running and instead hold lotteries or auctions for the remaining openings in Oklahoma. Most of the settlers were decent folk, as Fortson wrote, although the new county had plenty of trouble from its geography.

Its position on the edge of Indian Territory, where the line turned east along the Canadian River before heading north for forty miles, meant that Pottawatomie shared two long borders. One popular scheme was the horse-stealing racket. Fortson interviewed veteran officer John Hatfield, who described two trails that ran out of the county through Keokuk Falls in the north and Violet Springs in the south. "Stations" were set up every twenty-five miles where men could swap the horses they had stolen for new ones so that they could return "with another horse before his neighbors could become suspicious. The stolen horses would be taken on west by other riders, who, in turn, would ride back with horses stolen in the west."

As profitable as making off with horses was, a larger scheme was supplying the region with alcohol. Prohibition laws had made all of Indian Territory dry, but it was just a quick trip across the border to get all the drink one could want in Pottawatomie County. The bartending boom was said to have begun with a saloon in 1889, even though it wasn't until the later land runs that the area legally joined the Oklahoma Territory. The small town of Corner, which gained a post office in 1903, set up shop in the extreme southeast corner of the territory beside the Canadian River. Some speculate the name Corner came from a drawled pronunciation of the owner of the first saloon, Bill Conner's, name.

Others said the name was simply logical, as the town was located in the corner next to Indian Territory. While the saloons in Corner and Violet Springs did big business filling glasses, they also furnished visitors with plenty of alcohol to take with them. Some customers bought whole kegs, but the most fashionable—and less conspicuous—way to smuggle alcohol was to fill a couple of half-pint or pint bottles and tuck one into each boot. Jim Etter quotes Herman Kirkwood, a retired police officer, native of Konawa and local historian of Corner, as saying, "Bootleggin'—that's where it came from." Etymologists have traced the term back to 1889, the same time that Corner became a center for bootlegging, and they have traced its origins back to this region. Beforehand, a bootlegger was someone who smuggled weapons instead of booze.

Whiskey was a valuable commodity, since it was easily resalable, and local law enforcement had a habit of looking the other way. Kirkwood described that just about everyone was doing it as a matter of form, including a family that was going by wagon from Maud to Muskogee that brought along a barrel from Corner with them. "It was expensive, caring for the horses and all, and they sold whiskey up there and back to pay the expenses." In a letter to the *Tecumseh Republican* in 1898, W.J. Lackey lamented that Pottawatomie County had more arrests and prosecutions than any other county in the territory.

Along with the strong drink and easy money came plenty of violence. Conner was said to have gunned down two of his own patrons—one for merely asking too many questions. His saloon tallied an estimated fifty murders by 1905. The local doctor was kept busy stitching up bitten-off ears and cleaning gunshot wounds. Corner was credited by one newspaper as "one of the most unconscionable dives for hate and murder that ever existed in the Southwest," but it had plenty of company. All along the border, towns had their own saloons with plenty of visitors from the East. Keokuk Falls in the northeast corner of Pottawatomie was especially rowdy, since outlaws would slip across the border while hiding out in Indian Territory. The town boasted two distilleries, seven saloons and a carpentry shop dedicated to coffins. The story goes that the stagecoach driver whose route passed through the town would warn people, "Stop for twenty minutes and see a man killed." People say you can still see trees with bullets lodged in them in the area.

The achievement of statehood in 1907 ended the flow of alcohol, as the whole of Oklahoma became dry. Keokuk Falls, Corner and other watering holes faded into ghost towns. Fortson wrote that every business other than the saloons in Violet Springs packed up and moved to Konawa instead. If a town was to last, it needed a more permanent reason to exist than whiskey.

The biggest draw a city could have, most felt, was to be the county seat. It would be prime real estate, with a focus of legal and economic activity. Aspiring planners, like William Griffenstein, who had ensured that his wife's tribal allotment was situated in the estimated middle of what would become a county, looked to take advantage of this fact even before the run for the position had started. He turned the ranch there into a town called Burnett; there, he marked off lots to be sold and planned businesses. Griffenstein had helped found Wichita, Kansas, in a similar fashion by serving as a trader and then its mayor for over a decade beginning in 1878. Before the run, however, lobbyists pushed the federal government to rework the entire region so that six miles of the west would be given over to Cleveland County. Burnett, which was located eight miles south of today's Pink, was then far from the geographic center of the county, and the county seat went to Tecumseh—at least until the entrepreneurs at the long-established trading post called Shawneetown did something about it.

The rivalry between Tecumseh and Shawnee first climaxed with the railroad war. Railroads were the lifeblood of commerce—so much so that when the local line decided that it would put a stop in Asher but not in Avoca two miles to the north, the whole of Avoca moved two miles south to join it. The Choctaw, Oklahoma and Gulf Railroad was mapping its route west from Arkansas in 1890, and Tecumseh thought it would be a shoo-in for a stop as the county seat. However, the company wanted something in return: almost half the town lots as right-of-way property. Tecumseh refused, and the railroad decided to make a new route through the much more inviting Shawnee. Legal battles raged in local courts and Washington, D.C.—from the secretary of the interior to the U.S. Supreme Court—but the railroad persisted in heading west, through Shawnee. City father John Beard threw a champagne party for the whole town to celebrate the railroad's arrival on July 4, 1895.

Even though their cases in court were lost, Tecumseh citizens were determined to have their own railroad, so they built a line running toward Dale. The mail train ran back and forth twice a day, pulled by the town's famed engine, the *Lillian Russell*, except when it collided with a buggy in 1899 and had to be rebuilt in the shop over several days. The buggy only had to have its wheel replaced. Meanwhile, other citizens ensured that the Choctaw Railroad felt their vengeance by routinely torching and dynamiting bridges. One Shawneeite reciprocated by blowing up the north side of the county courthouse.

With the arrival of the railroad and the commerce it brought, Shawnee surged ahead in terms of population; it was already three times the size of Tecumseh by the time of the 1900 census. Politicians in Shawnee had their hearts set on moving the county seat as early as 1896. Tecumseh secured its hold on the offices in 1897 by supplying the funding for the new county courthouse and jail. Still, Shawnee fought on, finally winning a petition for a vote in 1909. Shawnee won that vote 8,024 to 5,027, but a later investigation showed bribery, and the results were thrown out. Another vote came in 1911, and this time, Tecumseh won out. Shawnee bided its time, but when the discussion began to build about constructing a modern courthouse in 1925, the county seat debate started up again. An election in 1930 gave Shawnee the victory by 11 votes, and this time, the supreme court decided in their favor, despite accusations of bribery, liquor and bringing in college boys to vote.

In the midst of the railroad war and the debates over the county seat, Pottawatomie County went to war with a phantom enemy in January 1898. It began with a horrific home invasion at the Leard residence, where two

An early-day parade celebrates on Main Street in Shawnee. *Courtesy of the Pottawatomie County Museum.*

men killed Mrs. Leard while her husband was away, finalizing their move to a new farm. No one knew a thing about it until seven-year-old Frank, while carrying his baby brother, walked the four miles into Maud the next morning to tell his neighbors. The possee found Mrs. Leard's body in the yard; her face and neck had been gnawed on by wild hogs. Their neighbor and landlord, Tom McGeisey, stated, "Killing's too good for a man who did this." A mob formed up around U.S. Marshal Nels Jones, and they tracked down the two men they believed had performed the murder. The men were found in the Seminole Nation, and when the mob grabbed them, they dragged them back to Oklahoma Territory, chained them to a tree and burned them to death.

The frontier justice brought little calm to the situation, which broiled along with the winter skies, which were alive with a series of strange thunderstorms. Fortson wrote that an old jokester named Sid Smith played on everyone's nerves by concocting a story that the Seminoles were forming up a war party to exact revenge on the whole county. One neighbor panicked and began fleeing on horseback, alerting everyone he could to the coming "attack." Soon, the towns of Maud and Remus were abandoned. In Tecumseh and Avoca, people fortified buildings and established a watch. Others throughout Pottawatomie County ran as far as Purcell. Many Native people in the county were fearful of reprisals, too, and hurried to the Seminole Nation to wait it out.

The terror came to a head when the railway agent at Earlsboro sent word out across the telegraph wires, calling for a militia. He said that he had just been told the attackers were coming into town and that he would abandon his post as soon as this last message went out. Men formed a makeshift army and rode the rail out to Earlsboro armed with whatever weapons they could grab—only to find an empty town and no sign of anyone invading but them. They ended up breaking into the locked-up train station to wait out the storm that night so that they could go home. Fortson noted that the only casualty of the "war" was Sid Smith himself, as the legend concludes that the deceived parties formed a new mob to string him up.

The federal government stepped in to restore order and arrested more than ninety people from the mob for the murder of the two burned men. Most were let go with minor punishments, although Marshal Jones was sentenced to twenty years for not stopping the mob. Another man later confessed to the murder, although newspapers at the time refused to believe him; they instead lamented the compensation that was granted from Indian affairs to the families of the men who had been killed.

The Wild West faded in Pottawatomie County as the twentieth century progressed. Cotton boomed as the major export, and industry, such as the historical Shawnee Mill, grew. Shawnee, especially, flourished, quadrupling in size by the time of the 1910 census. It also became a college town in the same year. The Benedictine monks who worked to rebuild Sacred Heart Mission in southern Pottawatomie after the disastrous fire of 1901 agreed to move their abbey to Shawnee and establish a school of higher education. A second college came to town when the 1910 Baptist General Convention of Oklahoma announced that it would create a "Baptist University of Oklahoma," today's Oklahoma Baptist University (OBU). Shawnee donated sixty acres and $100,000 cash to host the campus. While the economic struggles of the 1910s slowed the construction of the campus and even put a pause on classes, its first brick building was completed in 1915; it was dubbed Shawnee Hall in thanks of the city's support. The auditorium in the hall was later named for Rhetta Mae Dorland, who arrived in 1919 as the head of the expression department; there, she taught elocution classes and founded the College Players. Today, theater students whisper the legend that she still checks in on performances, appearing as a shadow in the back of the audience.

The region faced tough times in the 1920s, as pests wiped out the cotton crop, but things turned around with the beginning of the oil boom in 1926. Fortson wrote that there had been numerous attempts to find "black gold" in the early days; Pennsylvania Oil and Gas had even built test wells in 1903. Wells began to show promise in the mid-1910s, but the beginning of World War I stymied the chances for more exploration. It was not until oilman Joe Cromwell's car broke down in Seminole Nation in 1923 that a new wave of test wells was built, and these exploded with wealth. By 1930, Earlsboro alone had produced more than seventy-two million barrels of oil. The wave of oil money crashed into Pottawatomie County, along with a surge of immigrants who came to work the fields.

Fortson wrote that the property value in Shawnee tripled within the year. From 1927 to 1929, more than $1 million of construction was added to the town each month, including a municipal airport. All over the eastern part of the county, "garages were turned into bedrooms. Tents occupied every available space [and] oil shacks brought in high rents." Maud's population leapt from 1,500 to over 10,000, though this would drop by half as soon as the oil boom became stable production. When the oil boom did taper off in the mid-1930s, the feelings of the Great Depression settled in. Fortson wrote that Earlsboro, flush with income, had taken on debt for roads, "a $225,000 waterworks plant, and a $14,000 gym." The payments on these resulted in infamy after the oil prices dropped, as the town had the highest tax rate in the nation. It is a familiar ebb and flow; the oil tide periodically washes over the state with abundant cash, but that money dries up when oil prices drop.

Along with the oil prosperity, the county gained new notoriety for its lawlessness among the surging crowds of roughnecks. Many had returned to bootlegging in the heyday of Prohibition. U.S. district attorney Herbert K. Hyde patrolled the area, only to discover saloons and stills in every direction, distributing some eight thousand gallons of booze every three months to thirsty oilfield workers. More famously, the region became the hiding place for outlaws, including one of the most notorious of the gangster era, Charles A. "Pretty Boy" Floyd.

Floyd fled to Earlsboro after his legendary escape from a prison transport in Ohio in 1930. It was easy enough to hide among the newcomers, and Floyd had plenty of connections; his brother's family had settled there, and it was the hometown of Floyd's partner-in-crime, George Birdwell. Floyd hit banks all over Oklahoma in 1931 and 1932, including the Bank of Earlsboro, which he hit *twice*. After Birdwell's robbery at Boley turned to murder, Floyd headed out of the state, even though he wasn't a part of the

Fueled with oil money, Shawnee residents had plenty to invest in automobiles. *Courtesy of the Pottawatomie County Museum.*

job. He was eventually gunned down in 1934, but by then, his legendary status as a modern-day Robin Hood had taken hold, following the rumors that he would tear up poor farmers' mortgages while he robbed the banks. Woody Guthrie immortalized him with a song in 1939, in which he sang, "But a many a starvin' farmer, the same old story told, how the outlaw paid their mortgage and saved their little homes. Others tell you 'bout a stranger that come to beg a meal, underneath his napkin, left a thousand-dollar bill."

Theresa Cody related her father's story of meeting Floyd while he was gassing up the outlaw's car at the Earlsboro filling station, where he worked. Floyd beckoned the young man to come close and even join him in the car. Those were the days of famous kidnappings, such as the kidnapping of the Lindbergh baby and numerous Oklahoma oilmen, so the young man was a bit nervous of the outlaw's suggestion. After politely turning him down, he finished filling the gas tank and busied himself with checking the engine so that he could send Floyd on his way. It was not until later that he thought about how there would not be much of a ransom for a gas station attendant. Instead, he realized, "Pretty Boy Floyd was trying to slip me some money!"

Terry Isaacs told his grandfather's own stories about Floyd. Ben Isaacs, who had homesteaded a land run farm in Pond Creek, made the journey down to Earlsboro in the early 1930s to buy sheep as he built his flock. Since travel in those days required a great deal of waiting, Isaacs spent his time playing cards and joined in with Floyd. Over the years, people asked him if he was ever nervous and if he let the outlaw win. Isaacs replied, "Of course not! He's just a regular guy."

Today's Shawnee may seem calm in comparison with the frontier and Prohibition-era town, but the spirits of the past still persist in Shawnee. One café manager in the town told the tale of hearing voices in the back room of their restaurant. The event occurred after hours, long into the evening, as she was doing the accounting, yet she heard several distinct voices in the chatter. She heard silverware clinking against plates, and then, it sounded like every chair in the room scooted back, like they do at the end of a dinner party. She hurried to investigate and flipped on the light, but she found that the whole room was empty, not a single chair was out of place and all the tables were cleared.

Another restaurant claims that its previous owner makes appearances. He once lived in the apartment at the back of the shop, which is now used for offices. Instead of sticking around his home, it is believed he returns to work, as staff frequently hear different machines start up by themselves. Something unseen triggers the motion sensors on faucets and paper towel

Shawnee High School stands imposingly on its hilltop. *McCoy photograph.*

machines, and soda fountains spurt out regularly, as if the lines are being cleaned. While this can be startling, most of the staff say it's just a reminder of how dedicated he was to his work.

Other establishments also seem to have ghostly visitors. At one department store, people have reported hearing sounds in the back rooms that are now used for storage; this is not an uncommon event, and it could simply be the result of a large building settling. Items sometimes fall off shelves without anyone around, and this can result from unfelt vibrations in the ground. Shadow figures walking by may be tricks of the light. Yet, no one has an explanation for the handprints that appear on mirrors in closed back bathrooms, where only managers have the keys. Some have even tried to match the prints with staff, but they prove to be far too big to have come from anyone in the store. More strangely, words written by fingertips also appear in the dust on the mirrors; they sometimes reply to "hi" with "hello."

These are only the beginnings of Shawnee's haunted tales.

1
ARRIVED
THE AMERICAN INDIAN TRIBES OF SHAWNEE

One of the most common misconceptions of hauntings is that a new building without a traumatic past can't possibly have paranormal activity. Many don't stop to realize that a building doesn't have to exist for a haunting to occur. Many times, it's not a building at all that retains the history or haunting—it's the land that it sits on and the people who dwell there.

The Absentee Shawnee Tribe of Oklahoma originated in the eastern United States, where it occupied land that eventually became several states, including Ohio, Indiana, Illinois, Kentucky, Tennessee and Pennsylvania. The Shawnee were considered nomads, and they often traveled the length between Canada and Florida as they followed the animal populations. When the fur trade started to boom in their homelands, the Shawnee, like most other tribes, fought for the rights of trade. During the French and Indian War, the Shawnee found themselves fighting alongside the French, but the Anglo-Americans pushed onto their tribal lands. The Shawnee, along with ten other Native American tribes with ties to the Ohio Territory, joined together under the leadership of Tecumseh and his brother, the prophet Tenskwatawa, to resist the American encroachment. This uprising was ultimately defeated by General William Henry's army at the Battle of Tippecanoe in 1811, and the death of Tecumseh at the Battle of Thames in 1813 ended the united Native American front.

A new treaty, known as the Treaty of Fort Meigs, was signed in 1817. With this treaty, all Shawnee lands were effectively ceded to the federal government of the United States, and the Shawnee were forcibly moved to three reservations in Ohio. President Andrew Jackson later signed into law the American Indian Removal Act on May 28, 1830, forcing all Native Americans to move west of the Mississippi River. Later that same year, they were again forced to move to the Kansas Territory. In 1840, many scattered groups migrated to the Oklahoma Territory, where they settled along the Canadian River. Since they were considered absent for the Shawnee Tribe in Kansas, they collectively became known as the Absentee Shawnee Tribe.

In 1861, Kansas claimed its statehood and demanded that all Native American tribes be removed from their state; this forced the Native Americans to move, once again, to Indian Territory. The Kansas Shawnee joined the Absentee Shawnee and laid claim to acreage that was assigned to the Potawatomi. It took a congressional act in 1872 to title the lands to the Absentee Shawnee.

The Shawnee found new neighbors in the Citizen Potawatomi Nation. With ancestral homeland in the Great Lakes region, the Potawatomi Tribe was an Algonquin Native American people. The name Potawatomi means "people of the place of fire," which refers to their part in a long-term alliance called the Council of Three Fires. After several wars between their tribe and the U.S. government in the 1770s, the Potawatomi signed the Jay Treaty of 1794 and agreed to resolve their differences. Several more treaties

Shawnee settlers begin their lives in Indian Territory. *Courtesy of the Pottawatomie County Museum.*

were signed over the next several years, but it was the signing of the Detroit Treaty of 1807 that required the Potawatomi to relinquish some of their own lands. This caused outrage among many of the Potawatomi. Many became followers of the Shawnee prophet who went by the name of Tenskwatawa (1775–1836) and his brother, Tecumseh. The two brothers preached a doctrine of resisting the American expansion onto Native American lands. Their military alliance fought alongside the British during the War of 1812 and defeated the American garrison at Fort Dearborn in Chicago, but the Potawatomi fell on hard times after their defeat in 1814. Food became scarce, and they were left with little alternative but to exchange their land for money to ensure the tribe's survival. More treaties were signed over the following years, and in the 1830s, the Potawatomi were removed from their homelands and sent west of the Mississippi River. In 1838, the Potawatomi were forcefully removed from their Twin Lakes Village in Indiana to Kansas. The sixty-one-day march, which began on September 4 and stretched for approximately 660 miles, was known as the Potawatomi Trail of Death. That fall, 859 tribal members set out for Kansas; 49 died along the trail, most of them children.

On February 27, 1867, the Potawatomi signed another treaty; this one took them to a more permanent home in the Indian Territory, which is now known as Oklahoma. This group became known as the Citizen Potawatomie Nation and settled around the Shawnee area. Today, the Potawatomi Nation consists of more than thirty-three thousand tribal citizens. It is a federally recognized government and provides services to its citizens through many successful enterprises and revenues.

Like the Shawnee and Potawatomi, the Kickapoo originated from the Great Lakes region of Michigan and Ohio. In the 1700s, the Kickapoo split off into different bands and scattered throughout the region. It is believed that the Kickapoo and Shawnee were once part of the same tribe, as their languages are virtually identical. In 1819, each band signed a treaty that ceded their lands in Illinois to the United States government, but they did not adhere to the treaty and had to be forcefully removed. The next five years were considered the Kickapoo Resistance years, as many of the Kickapoo resisted acculturation into the White man's world and continued to migrate west toward Missouri. In 1832, another treaty was signed between the Kickapoo and the U.S. government, which allotted twelve square acres of land on a reservation in Kansas to the Kickapoo Nation. These lands, however, were swindled away by the railroad companies that looked to expand across the Kickapoo allotment. Homeless once again, the Kickapoo migrated into the Texas Territory and

North Mexico. After the Texas Revolution, the tribe found itself unwanted once more and was forcefully evicted in 1839. Some journeyed farther into Mexico, while others migrated into the Indian Territory.

The Kickapoo were assigned twenty-two thousand acres in the Oklahoma Territory, near McCloud. Between 1891 and 1893, the reservation was broken into individual allotments, but corruption ran rampant. A federal Indian agent who was in charge at the time illegally sold some of the Kickapoo allotments and was found guilty of the crime. Fraud over obtaining land allotments owned by the Native Americans was very prominent and often went unpunished. The abuse of power and greed had become so bad that many of the Kickapoo left Oklahoma to rejoin their fellow tribe members in Mexico. In 1883, a reservation was assigned to the remaining Kickapoo, but they, too, lost most of their promised land in the Allotment Act of 1893. In 1936, the Kickapoo tribe was federally recognized under the Indian Welfare Act, and its organization was officially formed. Today, the Kickapoo Tribal Headquarters of Oklahoma is located in McCloud, Oklahoma.

The Sac and Fox tribes also settled in what became Oklahoma. Though they are often grouped together, the Sac and Fox are not considered to be part of the same tribe. They are closely related in language and culture, but geographically and politically, they are quite different. Predominantly Sauk, the Fox and Sac Nation is the largest of the three federally recognized tribes of the Meskwaki and Sauk people.

The Sac (or "Sauk" as it was misspelled previously on a signed treaty) were called the "people of the yellow earth," a woodland culture group who lived in small villages and bark houses. Their people originated in Canada but later migrated farther south, into the Great Lakes region and, eventually, down into Kansas. The Fox, who were known as the "red earth people," were also considered part of a woodland culture and resided in the same type of villages and living establishments as the Sac. The Fox and Sac have a proud heritage and ancestral connection.

The tribes resided in Illinois from 1764 to 1830, but due to armed conflicts and the push of White settlers into their lands, treaties were signed, and they began to migrate into the Iowa region. They resided there from 1831to 1846, when they were once again pushed farther south to escape the White man's persecution. In 1847, they were sent into the Kansas Territory until Kansas gained its statehood and forced them to once again be removed from their lands and transitioned into Indian Territory, where they now reside. Today, one of their most well-known members is the famous Olympian Jim Thorpe, who is still considered one of America's greatest athletes.

During the Blackhawk War of 1832, the Sac and Fox faced the most notable conflict between their tribe and the U.S. government. The Sac and Fox joined Blackhawk, a Native warrior of the Sauk who led a dissident band of 1,000—500 of whom were warriors. The rest of the band consisted of women and children who were attempting to return to their native lands. Many were sick and injured from previous skirmishes; weak from hunger and lacking supplies, they faced a tragic end in the fall of 1832. On August 1 and 2 of that year, when the band of Native Americans attempted to cross the Mississippi River into the Wisconsin area, they were struck by cannon fire from a military ship as it unloaded its arsenal on their campsite on the beach. As the band of Native Americans faced the onset of cannon fire, another group of military soldiers charged from land. As many as 300 Sac and Fox tribal members took to the water, trying to canoe or swim across, only to be met by another enemy, the Sioux, a rival tribe. In the end, only 150 survived. The bodies of women and children were scattered across the blood-soaked ground, and the river ran red from the blood.

Blackhawk escaped death that day but later surrendered himself to the United States government on August 27. He was then taken to Washington, D.C., where he was introduced to President Andrew Jackson before being carted off to be used as a sideshow item in various eastern states, drawing large crowds wherever he went. The final blow to his pride occurred when he was handed over to his rival, Chief Keokuk.

Another accomplishment of the Sac and Fox Nation occurred on May 17, 1993, when the Supreme Court ruled to enforce the desire of the Sac and Fox Nation to have control over its own system for vehicle registration, despite the State of Oklahoma's fight against it. The idea was approached in 1983 but was not passed into law until ten years later. Since then, other tribes have followed suit, making themselves known wherever they drive.

In 1890, the Cherokee Jerome Commission, which was headed by David H. Jerome, met with the Absentee Shawnee, along with the Sac and Fox Nations, the Kickapoo, the Iowa and the Citizen Band of Potawatomi, to receive their allotments. Each tribal member received eighty acres, and the remaining land was sold back to the U.S. government. With the repurchase of land by the U.S. government, President Benjamin Harrison signed into effect a proclamation that authorized the second official land run in Oklahoma history. Many erroneously say that the settlement of Oklahoma began with the firing of a gun and a land run, but thousands of Native American settlers were already there.

As each tribe came into the region, their beliefs followed them, and each culture had its own collection of stories to share. The Native Americans, like many other cultural groups, have their own set of legends and folklore that have flourished throughout their long history, and they have traditions that have been passed down through the centuries through writings, songs and pieces of art. Many of the tribes share similar mythological creatures and beings; others have different versions of these mythological creatures or unique ones that are specific to their tribe. Some of the legends have been adapted, due to the influence of the Catholic religion and other Christianity-based beliefs that were taught to the Native Americans by missionaries who moved to the Oklahoma Territory. They all show great insight into Oklahoma's culture and land.

Many religions and legends contain one almighty entity or god. The Shawnee have Mishe Moneto or Mise Manito (along with several other spellings of the name), a great spirit that does not have any great attributes or a gender and is not personified in Shawnee folklore. For the Potawatomi, the name of their creator, or Great Spirit, is Kche Mnedo. The Wiske or Nanabozho, as it is known by the Potawatomi, is considered a benevolent hero of the Anishinaabe tribes. The name is spelled many ways, and there are a few different versions of the legend. Some claim the Wiske is the son of the west wind; others say he is the son of the sun. It is said that his mother died when he was a baby and that he was then raised by his grandmother Nokomis. He is considered a trickster but is also said to be a dedicated friend and teacher of humanity who never commits crimes or disrespects Native culture. Numerous human and demigod figures also appear in each tribe's folklore. Crazy Jack is a legend of the Shawnee Tribe; he is a jokester who is lazy and foolish but is usually able to get himself out of serious situations through moments of intuitive wisdom and good luck. The grandmotherly Kokumthena is considered a transformer or goddess.

The Sac and Fox share many of the same legends. One legend they have that is original to their tribes is the story of Lodge Boy and Thrown-Away. The twin boys were ripped from their mother's womb by a vicious monster named Two Faced while their father was out hunting. One boy was left inside the lodge while the other was thrown out into the yard. When he returned to the lodge, the father saw what had happened to his wife and unborn children. He was able to locate the child in the lodge, but the other remained alone until he was revealed by his brother. Lodge Boy was raised by his father in civilization while Thrown-Away grew up in the wild, untamed. Reuniting, the brothers avenged their mother's death and set out on monster-slaying adventures. Another version of the story states that Lodge Boy represents what is moral and that Thrown-Away represents the wickedness of the world.

The Kickapoo have many heroic legends as well, some shared, some specific to their tribal history. One such legend is that of the Wiza'ka'a. He is considered a benevolent hero and is sometimes referred to as a transformer. It is said that he was born of a virgin mother and is a good friend to mankind. He was raised by his grandmother, Mother Earth. He is considered a trickster and is often involved in humorous adventures.

One Potawatomi legend tells the story of Nanabozho and his war against the water serpent that stole his young cousin (or brother, depending on the translation), dragged him to the bottom of the lake—where he and his league of evil spirits resided—and killed him in the depths of the dark waters. It is said that Nanabozho sought revenge and called out to the Great Spirit to boil the waters and force the serpent onto land so that he might kill it. Soon, the waters began to boil, and the serpents sought refuge among the trees. Once they fell asleep, Nanabozho drew back his bow and sent an arrow flying into the serpent. He and his followers then returned to the lake; knowing that he was going to die, the serpent was determined to kill Nanbozho, so he caused the lake to swell and flooded the lands. Nanabozho ran back to his village to warn them that the serpent was angry and flooding the earth; he instructed them to run up the mountaintop. He then made a great raft from wood and saved as many people and animals as he could. It is said that the flood lasted for many days, while they remained on the raft until the waters finally receded. The serpent was dead, and his evil followers had returned to the dark waters below.

Chibiabos, who is also known as the Lord of the Dead, is Nanabozho's brother. Some stories portray him as the younger brother while others say they are twins. Still others claim they were not related at all and that Chibiabos was adopted. The name Chibiabos means "ghost rabbit," but it is said by some that he is a wolf spirit. Legend has it that he was murdered by a water spirit. His murder caused a violent chain of events that included the destruction of Earth by a great flood. It is said that, since he was unable to be brought back to life, he became the ruler of the underworld. He is portrayed as being a good and kind caregiver of the land of the dead.

Nambi-Za (Potawatomi), also known as the underwater panther, is considered to be a water spirit by many tribes and is often described as a water lynx, a powerful creature that resembles a cross between a cougar and a dragon. It is a dangerous monster that lives in the deepest part of the waters, often causing men and women to drown. Some legends say that it is the size of a mountain lion, while others claim it is enormous in size. It is often depicted as having the scales of a dragon in various colors. It is said to have a very long tail made of copper, horns or antlers and a saw-toothed back. The water serpent shows up in several tribal folklores and legends; many have the same descriptions but are known by a different name.

Another Native American water serpent is called Manetoa, or Mnito, and is known to the Sac (Sauk) and Fox Tribe as well as the Kickapoo. It is described as being a large snake-like creature, with horns and scales, that dwells in the bottom of lakes and rivers. It kills and eats men and women by dragging them to the bottom of the water. The only thing the Manetoa fear are the thunderbirds because they can kill them with their thunderbolts. The Kickapoo, too, have a similar tale about the Manetoa water serpents.

The legend of Deer Woman is also noted in several Native American cultures. She is considered a shapeshifter, which is fitting since some stories treat her as a sinister monster and others associate her with love and fertility. She is depicted as a woman who appears as a deer at times, and in other depictions, she is often a combination of both. In darker legends, she is described as a seductress, a woman scorned who leads promiscuous men to their deaths or leaves them pining for her with an insatiable lovesickness. Other versions of the story say that Deer Woman was a young woman who was raped and murdered; to find justice, she was brought back to life in the form of a deer that could appear as a woman. She enticed her murderers into the woods, one at a time, and trampled them to death with her hooves. Today, it is said she continues to hunt evildoers, luring them to their deaths. Some stories say the old Deer Woman was the one who resurrected the young Deer Woman, which suggests that there is more than one Deer Woman roaming around Oklahoma.

Perhaps the most famous figure of Native American folklore is the thunderbird. Cigwe' (more commonly spelled Chequa or Chequah) are known to the Potawatomi as thunderbirds or storm spirits, while the Shawnee call them Nemimkee. They are considered to be giant mythical birds that live in the sky, and it is believed that the flapping of their large wings is what produces the sounds of thunder. It is said that their gaze is fatal to humans but that they very rarely bother them. It is also said that they are protectors of mankind, especially against the water serpent.

Separate from the thunderbird, the Shawnee tell stories about another type of storm legend or spirit, cyclone person. It is said to have the dark tendrils of a tornado, which are described as being the long, flowing hair of the cyclone person. It is considered to be a kindred spirit of the tribe, not an antagonist, and is usually viewed in a positive manner.

Thunder beings, also known as Nenemehkia, are found in Kickapoo folklore. They are considered to be storm spirits that live in the sky and cause the thunder and lightning, making them dangerous spirits capable of killing mankind. The thunder beings are often described as having the form of a human elder, despite being depicted as large birds in most of the artwork. Like thunderbirds, they are also sworn enemies of the horned serpents and will rescue men from their clutches.

The Pa'is (also spelled Ba'is) is the name used for the little people in the Potawatomi culture. Not only do the legends of these creatures share similarities among the tribes of Pottawatomie County, but these magical little people are figures in just about every culture on Earth's folklore. They are considered to be nature spirits or spirits of the forests and are depicted as being approximately two feet tall. In comparison, they resemble the European version of gnomes. They are not usually considered dangerous unless they are provoked, but they do like to play tricks on people. The Kickapoo legends also contain a version of the little people called the Paissa (also spelled Piesiihia). These creatures are considered magical and mischievous, but they are usually considered benign nature spirits who like to play tricks. To this day, grandmothers will warn their grandchildren not to wander off by themselves or make too much noise when the little people are about.

Potawatomi people have several of their own creatures that they share with northern Anishinaabe tries, including the Nibiinaabe, which are a race of water spirits or mermen. Half man and half fish, these creatures live in the water and are often frightened by loud noises and humans. The Potawatomi also tell stories of the Wendigo, malevolent and evil man-eating giants. These creatures are considered the "bogey-men" of Potawatomi lore and legends; they are described as being large ice monsters with humans frozen inside of them where their hearts should be. Some legends say these monsters are created when a human commits a sin, such as selfishness, gluttony or cannibalism. Legend says that, in order to kill this creature, someone must be able to kill the human inside of them. Only then can the creature be defeated.

The Yakwawiak is a Shawnee man-eating monster that is said to resemble a stiff-legged hairless bear. Many believe the creature was inspired by woolly mammoths, as tribesmen used the word to describe elephants when they first saw the enormous animals at circuses. Yet, there are many different versions of this mythological creature's story.

A more modern bit of folklore tells the story of a large, humanoid creature with a wide wingspan that takes to the skies. Reports of this creature have come from Concho and Guthrie, as well as Shawnee. Jim Whitehead related a story from his research about a creature that was spotted behind the theater at the Shawnee Mall. Roughly six feet tall, it landed on a light pole and stared back at the people who had spotted it. Its body was the color of old, ratty leather, and it had red eyes that glowed from its rounded head. Then, it spread its wings and vanished into the night sky.

Could some of these creatures have existed long ago, frightening enough people for their stories and legends to withstand the test of time, or are these creatures still with us today, seen only by those with understanding eyes? Whether they are mystical or real, these stories continue to live on, bringing a greater reality to our world.

2
FROM THE ASHES
SACRED HEART MISSION

Few places in Oklahoma are greeted with as much excitement by visitors as Sacred Heart; this may be due to its urban legends, yet, its true story lends a greater depth to its reality. When the Citizen Potawatomi Tribe arrived in its new homeland in Indian Territory, it found itself without churches or religious leaders from the Catholic Church, the dominant religious group at the time. In France, new secular laws restricting religion in education prompted Benedictines, who had been teaching in the country for centuries, to move on. The two worlds met in 1876, when Father Isodore Robot responded to the call for aid from the Potawatomi. He and tribal leaders worked to obtain a land grant that would fund a mission and school. In the valley below Bald Hill, four miles north of the Canadian River, on timberland that was watered by two creeks, they began building log cabins and farming the land.

The mission flourished. More monks, as well as five nuns from the Sisters of Mercy, journeyed to aid Robot; Potawatomi children were enrolled in the boarding school, and older citizens were enrolled in Robot's technical institute. The mission had a school for boys and St. Mary's Academy for girls. In 1884, the education available at the mission took another step forward with the establishment of Sacred Heart College. Along with the schools came all of the supporting structures, including barns, sheds, a bakery, staff homes and a working farm with livestock, orchards and fields. From necessity, the mission also established two cemeteries: one for the

Left: A memorial stands at Sacred Heart for Saint Kateri Tekakwitha (1656–1680), the Lily of the Mohawks. *McCoy photograph.*

Below: A diorama shows the expansive Sacred Heart Mission in its heyday. *Provine photograph.*

Sisters of Mercy and one for the Benedictine monks. By 1882, the mission had grown into a full abbey, with Father Isodore elected as the first prefect apostolic in the Indian Territory.

Just after midnight on January 15, 1901, a fire broke out at the mission. It had been a dry winter, and strong winds that night drove the flames from one building to the next. The dormitories, school buildings and even the church burned, leaving only a few small buildings on the outskirts of the mission. Miraculously, no one was killed. The mission was rebuilt, but the territory had changed radically in the two decades since its founding. It was now located in the Oklahoma Territory, and railroads wound their way through the Cross Timbers. The needs of the land had changed. In 1903, the Sisters of Mercy, who had restarted their academy, moved to Oklahoma City, where land had been donated for a school for Catholic girls in the burgeoning new town. The new Mount Saint Mary's stood on a hill south of the river; for years, it was one of the only landmarks on what would become Capitol Hill.

The monks also moved on. Shawnee offered land for a Catholic university, and in 1929, the abbey was relocated to the campus grounds as well. Sacred Heart continued as a church on the hilltop, watching over the Sacred Heart Cemetery, which serves as a resting place for Catholics in the region. Many of the buildings from the old mission in the valley below have been torn down, but two still remain: a two-story cabin and the bakery. The site is listed in the National Register of Historic Places and open for guided tours of the grounds, which still feature the cemeteries and foundations of the original mission.

Some journey to Sacred Heart for another reason: ghosts. Steeped in history, the site holds onto many of its former residents, who are believed to watch over what they built. Visitors frequently collect electronic voice phenomena (EVPs) of sounds that are unheard by the human ear; these are most often collected near the cemeteries where the monks and sisters lie. The recordings carry the distant sounds of singing in French or Latin. Others have heard their names called but could not find anyone who could have called out to them.

While many who visit Sacred Heart do so legitimately, during its touring hours, it has also become a hotspot for less noble visits. Teenagers seeking adventure in rural Oklahoma have gone to the mission for generations to scare one another or to try to witness something truly supernatural. Whispered urban legends tell of the spirits of children who were massacred by the flames in 1901 still haunting the site, despite contemporary records

Left: An angel offers holy water at Sacred Heart Church. *McCoy photograph.*

Below: Two buildings and a few foundations still stand at the old Sacred Heart Mission. *Provine photograph.*

Sacred Heart Church stands on the hilltop above the mission valley. *Provine photograph.*

stating that no one perished. Yet, many who have been to Sacred Heart after dark claim that they have heard screams and cries in the night. The location that is most famous for the sounds of crying is the children's portion of the cemetery, where several groups have captured EVPs of wailing in the night. One woman said that, once, she and her friends snuck down the road as teenagers and were frightened by something else: eyes in the woods. They all had the eerie feeling of being watched. Glowing red eyes seemed to follow them, moving if the teens came too close. "It's just reflections of the brake lights," they assured themselves; yet, the eyes continued to glare at them, even after they had shut the car off. The teens did not stay long.

Another urban legend about the old mission, one linked to the famous grave of Katherine Cross in nearby Konawa that reads "murdered by human wolves," says werewolves are said to roam the Cross Timbers. Many believe these thick oaks near the river hide creatures without explanation. Tellers of the tale say that the strange sounds and glowing red eyes in the woods are actually signs of the lurking beasts. Some people have even ventured into the woods; there, they said they spotted a dark figure, roughly seven feet tall, lumbering between the trees. A young man who had once gone there with friends described the time he was chased by a spectral bull. He said it was gray with shining red eyes and that the air shook with its bellowing. The friends watched it stagger and rear in the moonlight, coming closer until it noticed them. Then, it went after them, chasing them all the way back to their truck. Once they were inside, the bull vanished, and they left quietly. Feeling guilty the next day, the young man went back to the farm next door to confess and let the farmer know that his bull had gotten out. The farmer told him that he hadn't run cattle in that field for months.

Parapsychologist Logan Corelli stated that, during an investigation with his team, they were sitting inside the basement of one of the restored buildings when they heard loud clanking from outside. It sounded as if someone was dragging heavy chains. Hurrying out to see what could have been making the noise, they found that the mission grounds were empty. Even so, the clanking sounds of chains rang on. Their investigation turned up several more phenomena, both visible and invisible. White light flashed from time to time, appearing brightly only for a moment before disappearing. They hunted for sources of the light, such as gas, but could not find anything. Nor could they find a material explanation for the cold spots that lingered in the cemetery on an otherwise hot summer night.

Sacred Heart is truly a place of powerful history. Unfortunately, vandals have struck over the years, destroying the precious remains of what once thrived there. Anyone who wishes to visit the site today must contact the gatekeeper at Sacred Heart Church to schedule an escort for a tour.

3

The Iron Key to Success

Arrival of the Railroad

Among the settlers who ran for land in 1891, there was a man named Mr. John Beard, who claimed the area that later became known as Shawnee. Beard knew that, for the area to prosper, they would need the railroad to come, so he, along with a group of fellow settlers, approached the Choctaw, Oklahoma and Gulf Railroad in hopes of convincing it to route its line through Shawnee. Mr. Beard even offered to give them part of his claim free of charge to sweeten the deal. Snubbed by Tecumseh, the railroad was happy to oblige. Only July 4, 1895, hundreds of people showed their support by waving and cheering as the first Choctaw engine arrived in Shawnee. Beard led the celebration with a champagne party for the whole town. The celebration continued with the town's prosperity. Not only did the Choctaw Line bring the first railroad to the area, but it also decided to make the town the location of its repair shops, bringing in jobs and establishing a whole district of workshops in Shawnee.

Two of the other major railways soon entered the Shawnee area: the Missouri-Kansas-Texas Line (M-K-T, also known as the "Katy") and the Rock Island Railroad. The Katy was first chartered in the state of Kansas when the government announced the new right-of-way law through the Indian Territory and with liberal bonuses of land for being the first railroad to reach the northern border. Major investors like J.D. Rockefeller were quick to jump on board, even though the land grant was overturned by the courts when they ruled that Congress had overreached when attempting to grant Native American lands to the railroad. The Rock Island Railroad

Shawnee celebrates its railroad history on Main Street with a special parade. *Courtesy of the Pottawatomie County Museum.*

entered the Indian Territory, traveling north and south, and it soon set its sights on obtaining the Choctaw east–west lines, especially since the two lines intersected in El Reno. On May 6, 1902, with the funds in hand, the Rock Island Railroad was able to obtain the documents it needed to purchase of the Choctaw Railroad Line.

With its railroads, Shawnee flourished. By 1902, Shawnee had several cotton gins and two cotton presses and was shipping out 375 railroad cars full of cotton product each day. In 1903, a streetcar system was set in place. In 1907, Shawnee played host to an average of 42 passenger trains and 65 freight trains daily, rivaling even Oklahoma City.

Not only did the arrival of the railroad bring life to the town of Shawnee, it also brought some tragedies. One such disaster claimed the lives of many and changed the face of the historic Rock Island Shops forever. Located at the end of Union Street, the area was a busy hub for businesses and passengers alike and became the largest railway shop in the Southwest. Not only are they remembered for their sheer size, but they were also marked by a devastating explosion during the height of the holidays. Just after noon on December 24, 1909, an employee of the railroad had just completed some repairs on engine no. 1830. As the engine was being fired up, the boiler exploded, propelling it into the west side of the shop, and the firebox of the engine was hurled through the north brick wall. The employee who had been working on the engine was not seriously injured, since he was safely in the pit under the engine when it exploded. The explosion extended outward, however, and claimed the lives of many that day.

Two of the victims were a machinist and a fireman. Reports said they were "blown to atoms," as they took a direct hit during the explosion. Also among the dead were Henry Johns, a twenty-year-old man who left behind a wife, and A.F. Kerry, a single man who had just saved up enough money to open his own business in Iowa. He was planning on moving to Iowa on New Year's Day, but little did he know that he would never live to see the end of the year. Several more were seriously injured.

People were frantic as the news spread. The first reports of the numbers of injured and deceased were much higher than the actual numbers, and

Hundreds came out to cheer on the new railroads of Shawnee. *Courtesy of the Pottawatomie County Museum.*

they caused many friends and family to flock to the area. The national guardsmen were ordered by Governor Haskell to assist Fire Chief Brown and Police Chief C.C. Hawk to help maintain order and control the crowds. The day was spent looking for survivors as well as the deceased. Reports said that body parts were scattered all over the scene and on the tops of some of the nearby buildings. The survivors of the explosion were treated in various locations, including at the Shawnee Hospital, but the more seriously injured victims were taken to the Rock Island Hospital in McAlester. Even though many were injured and some were killed, the disaster could have been much more catastrophic. Had it not been lunch time, an average of 250 workers would have been in the area during the explosion.

Emotions run high with any disaster, especially if there is a sudden loss of life. Energy is fueled by the accident and imprints are made on time. Could this incident have fueled the paranormal activity in and around the Shawnee area? Do the spirits of this disaster still haunt the railways today? Tanya, along with a few of her fellow paranormal investigators, decided to visit the location at the end of Union Street, where the incident had taken place. They sat in their vehicles (since it was a very cold evening) and attempted to run a ghost radio session to see if they could contact some of the victims from that tragic accident. Their method of investigation used a device that scans radio frequencies to interpret the electronic white noise that is believed to be a carrier for spiritual communication. When they asked if there was anyone there who would like to speak with them, one name did come across: Henry. Tanya asked if he had died in the incident, but no response was given. She then asked if he was injured in the incident; immediately, they received the word "paralyzed." They concluded their quick investigation of the site and thanked the spirits for talking to them. With such a tragic accident resulting in the death and injury of so many, evidence of spirits still lingering around this location shsould not be surprising. One can only hope that, one day, the spirits that continue to linger on this earth will find peace and happiness in the afterlife.

The explosion of 1909 is not the only tragedy linked to the rails. Various accidents and injuries have occurred there throughout the years, leaving many to wonder if the resulting spirits still wander the lonely tracks on cold, dark nights. There are a few stories of shadowy apparitions walking the tracks that surround the railways of Shawnee. Many workers and people driving by have seen them walking around, only to watch them suddenly disappear before their very eyes. Shocked, the witnesses look back, but no one can be found. One of Shawnee's most famous tales is that of the

Railroaders say farewell on the last run of the Santa Fe Passenger Line. *Courtesy of the Pottawatomie County Museum.*

conductor who is sometimes seen standing on the platform of the railway station. It is said that people see him standing there, as if he is waiting for the next train to pull into the station. One second he is there, and then he disappears in the blink of an eye. Perhaps this conductor and the figures on the tracks are all waiting for the arrival of a ghostly train that continues to ride the rails, hoping to find its glory days once again.

Another story associated with the historic railways of Shawnee is that of a special canine by the name of Bo who loved to ride the rails. Bo was never one to stay home; a regular hobo, this black-and-white spotted dog often caught himself a ride by hopping in a freight car. Despite his owner trying to keep him fenced in, Bo would always find a way out; he would always head down toward the railyard to catch a ride out. He would often follow the night yardmaster and catch a ride on the Boomer car that hauled men to all the shop buildings. The passengers soon became very fond of the dog and started to call him Bo (short for the name of the car he liked to ride so often).

Today, the tracks in Shawnee host shadowy figures that are said to be the victims of accidents that occurred long ago. *McCoy photograph.*

Soon, Bo became a regular assistant around the yard. He often helped herd animals into the freight cars—one of his favorite pastimes.

One day, tragedy struck. Bo spotted a sow's ear sticking out of one of the slats in the freight car; he grabbed for it but fell, landing under one of the train's wheels, which severed the lower part of one of his paws. After recovering, Bo became a real traveler. He was often seen as far away as Newton, Kansas, and Gainesville, Texas, sitting beside the engineer or riding along in the caboose. Bo could no longer jump up on the platform due to his injury, so the workers helped to lift him up. Bo spent the rest of his days riding the rails across Oklahoma before passing away in 1921. In honor of his days on the rails, many of the people who knew and loved him pitched in to make a special copper box for him to be buried in. He was laid to rest behind the yard office, next to his favorite place on earth, the railroad.

4

Shawnee's First Ghost

The Murder of Mollie Colclasure

A bold headline stood out in the May 12, 1909 issue of the *Shawnee Daily Herald*: "MURDERED IN A LONELY PASTURE." Mollie (sometimes "Molly") Colclasure was a widowed mother of three who lived at the American Rooming House on South Union Avenue. Colclasure was using Shawnee as a stop on her way to Chandler, where her relatives lived. She had previously lived in Shawnee several times, finding work in the bustling city, the fifth largest in the state. Her life ended abruptly on May 10, 1909, in a mystery that remains unclear to this day.

The *Herald* explained, "The body of the dead woman was discovered yesterday morning at 6 o'clock in the McConkey pasture, southeast of this city, by the owner of that place." McConkey immediately contacted the police, but they already knew. The night before, twenty-one-year-old Claude Garman (sometimes "Claud Gorman") had been Colclasure's companion as she took a stroll through the farmlands outside of town. Their night was interrupted, as the article says, when a "third party…intruded with a six-shooter." The man said, "I know you, Lindsey. You get out of here, or I'll kill you." The couple dashed in opposite directions, hoping to escape. Garman heard shots and believed that one was aimed at him. He managed to get out of the gunman's range and headed immediately for Shawnee. There were sounds of another shot behind him, but he didn't go back to check. Instead, Garman sought safety in numbers, which meant getting to town.

When he arrived there, he waited, looking to see if Colclasure had come after him. She had not, so he went to her boardinghouse to check if she

Even though it was only a few years old in this photograph, Shawnee was already an expansive city. *Courtesy of the Pottawatomie County Museum.*

had gone home. The article states, "She was not to be found." At 9:30 p.m., Garman went to the police to give a report. Two officers, Detective Darden and Assistant Chief Spann, followed him back out to the pasture. There was "no trace of the woman…to be found." Police decided to send Garman on his way. It was not until the next morning that McConkey found her body fifty yards from where they had been searching. Her body was still wearing Garman's coat from the night before. Inside the pockets "were letters that told of her deep love for Garman." While there was an issue with who the city coroner was at the time since there had been an election and the new coroner had not yet been instated, there were no disagreements on what had happened to Colclasure. "An autopsy will not be held, as there is no question as to how the deceased came to her death. Her head was pierced with a .45-calibre bullet, entering at the left cheek. The face was badly powder burned, showing that the shot was fired at close range. The arms and other parts of the body were badly bruised."

Garman reported back to the police that morning and gave the same statement to the desk sergeant and police chief, who decided to hold him in a cell. Interviews by police and a reporter from the *Herald* quickly found people to corroborate Garman's story. Nearby residents said that they heard the shots—first a volley and then a final shot some fifteen minutes after. Two boys said that they saw a man run by them soon after hearing the shots. They then saw two men in the dark pasture "attempting to corral the horses as though they intended to lead them off. They were unsuccessful and gave up the task."

Questions arose about a horse theft gone awry, but the police focused on the possible motive of a jilted lover. Colclasure had been engaged to one Ambrose Craine on and off in the past. Police went to interrogate Craine, but he was nowhere to be found. He was the primary suspect until the police were able to track him down; he had become a teacher at a school eight miles north of Wewoka. Craine came to town to give his statement, proving with numerous witnesses that he was at a meeting on the other side of the Seminole nation until 10:00 p.m. that night.

Shawnee was by no means a quiet town. The same front page that announced Colclasure's death showed an article of a bombing at the offices of the waterworks during a city council meeting. There were plenty of other cases of violence to deal with in the town, and police needed to close the books on such a notorious murder. Claude Garman was ultimately charged with Colclasure's murder and was held without bail, despite his cooperation with police. During the trial, his story never changed. The prosecution focused on his lack of detail in the description of the man who had attacked them; he described him as being medium in height, with a heavy build and dark complexion. Garman insisted that was all he could see due to the dim night. The defense brought forth ample evidence to show that Garman and Colclasure were genuinely in love, as he had followed her to Shawnee after meeting her in their previous residence in Hotulke. Garman insisted that he had never even owned a .45 revolver. Still, the jury became hung, and the trial was taken to a higher court. Ultimately, Garman was found guilty of murder and sentenced to life imprisonment.

Seemingly, this was the end of the story. Mollie Colclasure was buried in Chandler, where her children were taken in by their grandparents. Yet, rumors began to circulate in Shawnee that Colclasure's murder could be witnessed by anyone who was brave enough to venture into the pasture where it took place. On certain nights, her ghost would replay the violence. The story went that Mollie Colclasure's phantom would appear from thin air, running desperately northward. Behind her, the apparition of a large, dark man manifested. He chased her noiselessly with an outstretched revolver, growing closer and closer until he grabbed her and dragged her to the ground. He would then place the gun against her cheek and pull the trigger. Then, the vision would vanish.

In January 1911, the *Shawnee Daily News* printed a story about some young people who decided to investigate the apparition for themselves one wintry night. "They entered the pasture, but being somewhat timid at the outset, kept near the outskirts." While they were skulking about, McConkey's neighbor, Pleas Lain, noticed the bunch out in the pasture. He had recently been the victim of a burglary in which the thief had made off with his dinner while he was out, and he thought these young people might have been the same culprits "or someone else with evil intent." He called to one of his neighbors, who came up after him. The article noted that Lain was wearing his long undershirt and was "a good sprinter," which "gave the appearance of a white-clad figure easily mistaken for a woman being pursued by a man." The would-be teen investigators were surprised to the point that "the girls began to scream, panic stricken, and the boys are said to have stood speechless with fear." Lain revealed himself not to be a ghost, and the newspaper assured readers that no spirits would soon be bothered in that pasture.

While Garman's family continued to petition for his parole and pardons from jail, the mystery of what actually happened that night grew when almost the exact same murder happened again. The citizens of Shawnee began to notice that there was an astonishing trend in the murders that occurred south of town throughout the years. In 1906, just east of Tecumseh, the body of a young man was discovered in a buggy, "and the girl who had accompanied him was lying dead about a quarter of a mile away." The murder weapon had been a large-caliber gun. Even though the weapon could not be found, the police at the time decided that the event was a murder-suicide. A short time later, Charles McDaniels and his companion were attacked. He was shot in the back, which left him crippled for the rest of his life. His girlfriend was "dragged away into the bushes" but survived the assault. Her description of her assailant matched Garman's.

In September 1910, Victoria Page; her companion, Mr. Shifflett; her daughter, Irene McKinney; and Irene's boyfriend, Willie Canallis (often "Willie Vaughan"), were crossing by a pile of brush near Benson Park one night when Mrs. Page was "shot through the body and killed" with a .45-caliber bullet. Canallis was convicted of the murder, even though he only owned a small-caliber revolver that he had left at home that night. Then, in December 1910, Jessie Eddington was discovered unconscious but alive in a ditch near Benson Park. Her boyfriend, Charles Robarts, had led locals to her, saying that they had been attacked while lying together in a wagon. Robarts claimed that he had been hit twice by a wagon spoke, which dazed him and caused him to run east. Eddington had run in the opposite direction, and the assailant followed her. Robarts recovered enough to draw his gun, but he had lost track of Eddington and the attacker. Instead, he went for help and brought armed men back with him, only to find Eddington alone and severely injured. She later recovered in the hospital, and Robarts was eventually convicted of staging an attack.

On the night of September 3, 1911, Clifford Hughes was riding home from Benson Park with his younger sister, Oneta, when their horse's harness broke and left them stranded. He got out to inspect the horse and found the harness had been cut systematically with a knife. They had started walking home when a man stepped out from the edge of a bridge and shot Clifford. Oneta screamed and ran into a cotton field, but she was caught and beaten with the gun. The sound of gunfire brought neighbors out to see what was happening, but the assailant had left by then. Though both Hugheses were rushed to the hospital, neither survived long after giving their statements of being attacked by a strongly built man of medium height who had a dark complexion.

Concerned citizens rallied around a theory that had risen from the similarities in the crimes; the widespread belief was that they were all the work of one maniac, possibly with an accomplice. Fundraisers promised $1,000 in reward for the capture of this maniac, but the trail soon went cold, as the murders had tapered off. It wasn't until 1915 that the police announced they had caught the criminal: one Ed Berry. Berry held up George Myers and Jemima Barto on the east side of Shawnee with an automatic pistol, robbed Myers of $4.50, attacked Barto and then slipped away into the brush. From the victims' reports, police identified Berry and picked him up, finding one of Myers's silver dollars in his pocket. Interrogations suggested he had been responsible for other attacks throughout the years. Before Berry could go to trial, however, a mob stormed the jail and lynched him.

Officials claimed to have written confessions for the previous murders, but the lack of an evidence trail tied the hands of the legal officials, and they were unable to release those who were convicted earlier. Some believed that Berry was indeed responsible for all of the crimes, but others felt that Berry's holdup was not at all like those that came before, in which victims had been killed rather than robbed. They felt he was innocent, like Canallis, Robarts and Garman, meaning the true maniac was still on the loose. With all of the swift and questionable convictions, suspicions arose over whether this maniac was somehow politically protected. Perhaps the truth of these serial murders from over a century ago will never be clear. The tragedies themselves are at least known, replayed again and again, as Mollie Colclasure's phantom repeats her last moments in the lonely pasture, running in terror from a murderer who struck with no more reason than to kill.

5

Woman in the Window

The Shawnee Governor's Mansion

It may seem strange for a town that has never been the capital to have a building known as the Governor's Mansion. Hopeful residents of Shawnee thought so, too, so its construction was made part of their strategy to become the capital of the future state of Oklahoma. After securing the railroad, city leaders determined that they could further the town's growth and help increase the economic wealth for the city by bagging the capital.

Guthrie had been the capital of the Oklahoma Territory since its organization in 1890, but promoters in Oklahoma City had called its position into question from the beginning. To help secure their hold on the capital, the citizens of Guthrie pooled their resources to build a legislature building, which, today, is attached to the Masonic temple in town. Still, Oklahoma City urged a move, preferably southward. Residents who lived in and around the Shawnee area thought it could move a bit more east as well. In the hopes of securing the title, the citizens of Shawnee decided to build a grand mansion that was to be offered as the residence for the governor of Oklahoma. Several of the town's most prominent civic leaders donated both land and money to help fund the project.

Construction began in 1903 in the area known as Shawnee's first neighborhood, which was located northwest of downtown. Built in a southern plantation design, a nonclassical architectural style, this two-story home came equipped with two formal living rooms (one for men and one for women), a full basement, an attic, indoor plumbing, a grand kitchen and

The Governor's Mansion that never hosted a governor. *Provine photograph.*

multiple bedrooms. Tall Ionic columns decorate the east and south sides of the home, and a turret adorns the third story. The home boasts twelve-foot ceilings and many wide bay windows.

Despite the grandeur of the home, Shawnee was not chosen to become the capital of the new state; it came in with over eight thousand votes in the election of 1910, but it was still far behind Guthrie and the winner, Oklahoma City. Hopes that others would join with Shawnee in upsetting both of the big competitors were dashed when the votes came in with a large margin supporting Oklahoma City. While Guthrie fought the election all the way to the Supreme Court, Shawnee bowed out. The Governor's Mansion was sold to a private owner, a man who went by the name of Zygund O. Giza, and the house was renamed the Giza House for most folks in town. Despite the renaming of the home, other people still knew it—and will forever know it—as the Governor's Mansion, even though no Oklahoma governor has ever lived there. Even the National Register of Historic Places, which granted protected status to the house in 1983, knows it as the Governor's Mansion.

Today, the house is still owned by a private citizen and is currently split into a two-family home, with one of the current residents having lived there for the past forty years of her life. Stories of the home being haunted are shared among some of the residents who live around the area. With its long and famous history, the Giza House has also earned a reputation for being haunted. The most famous report is of a ghostly woman who stands in the attic window, looking out over the street. Passersby glance up to see a figure, usually in a white dress, gazing out as if she is taking in the eastward view of the town. Taking another glance, they lose sight of her and instead see only the aging skeleton of the once-grand mansion.

One of the residents of the home stated in an interview that he had not had any personal experiences of any possible paranormal activity. He did, however, relate the story of the woman peering out of the attic, whom many people have shared with him. There is no explanation as to who she may be or why she may be still residing in the home, but those who drive by make sure to look up to see if they might be lucky enough to catch a glimpse of the ghostly lady in the window.

6

Glimmers of the Past

Haunts of Downtown Tecumseh

Following the land run of 1891, downtown Tecumseh became the legal and economic center of what would become Pottawatomie County. Entrepreneurs, along with those who did not necessarily have a plan of how to make money but hoped that being near the middle of it all would make them rich, poured their resources into the town. Stories from after the run tell of one man who hurried to dig the first well in town and then sold water for $0.05 per cup ($1.45 in today's money). He was kinder to horses; they could get a whole bucket to drink for a dime. Another businessman, John Black of Noble, was legally too young to make the run himself, as he was just a teenager, but he figured he could make some money as well. After buying a wagonload of one-by-fours from the lumberyard in Norman, he drove it to Tecumseh, where he resold them at $1.00 apiece for a tidy profit. Demand was so strong for just about anything that the first bakery in town, which was run by Hibbard and Smith, had to nail its windows shut to fend off mobs gathering at the scent of their first batch of bread.

As the town became settled, so did its residents—for the most part. For over a year, Tecumseh would struggle with its most infamous residents: the Christian Brothers Gang. Bob and Bill Christian were wild cads who frequented the saloons between Corner and Keokuk Falls. They started their careers in crime as petty thieves, and many suspected them of being members of the horse-thieving ring that had sprung up in the early county. Their thieving turned to murder as the brothers more frequently visited the saloons, and their path took a darker turn in 1895, when Deputy Sheriff

Will Turner went to collect them. Instead of going quietly, Bob and Bill gunned him down near Violet Springs. A posse formed up to pursue them, and after three weeks on the run, the two gave up in the hope of receiving clemency. Their hopes were dashed by a vengeful judge, and the Christians found themselves in the Oklahoma City Jail, waiting for an appeal that would decide their fate.

Taking that fate into their own hands, the brothers managed to have a female acquaintance sneak revolvers to them in their cell, where they teamed up with their cellmate, Jim Casey, who was also being held on a murder charge. The three shot their way out. Though Casey was gunned down just outside the jail, the Christians made their escape back to Tecumseh. Lawmen began rounding up known accomplices, which led them to the Christians' father's house, where Bob and Bill had been hiding out. A posse of lawmen traded over fifty gunshots with them, but the Christians managed to escape yet again—this time, over the border into Indian Territory. The story goes that they continued on the run to Arizona Territory, where they were both eventually gunned down.

Even in the early days of Tecumseh, ghost stories cropped up. Area newspapers reprinted an editorial that warned of a scheme to get lower rent, especially in regions like Pottawatomie County, where plenty of newcomers relied only on word-of-mouth for recommendations on where to live. The article read, "The newcomer takes a house and, after one or two payments of rent, complains that the premises are haunted. Quaking with simulated fear, he tells a tale of horror—of a headless man seen stalking from the coal cellar, a lady in white or of something invisible but groaning." It goes on to say that, while ghost stories are good enough for neighborhood gossip, landlords should want to avoid them at all cost. "Anxious that the report shall not get about, landlord confers with tenant, and in several such instances the result has been this—the tenant agrees to stay on, to say nothing about the matters to others and to put up with the ghost, providing the rent is substantially reduced." While the ghosts in such schemes were dreamed up, others made themselves known to innocent witnesses, and their histories live on in the stories today's citizens tell.

One focus of Tecumseh's history is the old Farmers Bank building, which once stood on the northeast corner of the intersection of Park and Broadway Streets. For decades, its turret and large second-floor windows looked proudly over the community it helped build. The building grew up from the ashes of the January 1906 fire that wiped out a whole block of downtown, from the Hames Studio to Weatherington's Shoe Store,

Blakeney & Connor Law Offices and the previously wooden bank building. Farmers Bank, which had grown by leaps and bounds since its establishment in 1902, had already been planning to construct a new brick building. The bank partnered with the local lodges of the International Order of Odd Fellows and Masons that were in need of meeting space. Within weeks, the straw-colored buff brick walls with white stone trimmings stood on the corner. The interior took longer to complete, as the workers dedicated themselves to affixing plate glass, laying tile and installing a burglar-proof manganese vault downstairs, all while lathing a lodge room for the fraternities upstairs.

Through the years, even after the bank was closed, its namesake building remained busy, hosting businesses such as the McMahon Grocery and Shackleford's Shoe Repair. Even when it became vacant toward the end of its days, the building still carried an energy of the people who had once visited it so often. At least two people are recorded as having died there. One death was accidental and occurred when Dane Dixon fell down the stairwell to meet his end. The other was more violent; in 1928, the building's night watchman, Grover Butler, was killed by what local news called an "undesirable." Whether the spirits of these men remained or the building contains residual energy that replays itself, the Farmers Bank building gained a whispered reputation of being haunted. People claimed, from time to time, to see lights on upstairs, although skeptics said the light came from the old windows reflecting a streetlight from somewhere unseen. The skeptics have had less to say about the sounds of footsteps that can be heard walking up and down the stairs. To hear a creak of a building settling at night is one thing, but the consistent *thud-thud-thud* of heavy shoes is something else entirely. People in the empty building often pursued the sound, thinking someone else had slipped in, but thorough searches revealed no body to go along with the sound.

The Farmers Bank building was torn down in 1982, but there are plenty of other legends of ghosts that remain down the block in the old opera house. The Tecumseh Opera House was opened on September 22, 1905, with a showing of *Alabama*. The crowd was estimated to be five thousand people, although it is uncertain where they would have put everyone. The opera house's lower floors featured a wide lobby and numerous offices for a variety of businesses; these led up to the third-floor theater, where seven hundred people could enjoy a show. This was the focus of entertainment for the town; it hosted vaudeville shows, Chautauqua lectures and, according to some, seedier late-night romps.

The Tecumseh Opera House stands solemnly, a shadow of its former glory. *Provine photograph.*

Through the years, the opera house was kept busy hosting numerous different companies. At different times, the building's office space served the telephone company and city post office. When movie theaters brought an end to opera houses, the Tecumseh Opera House was revived as hotel space for the Marnie and, later, the Central Hotel. Trade in this industry also dried up as the years went on, and the opera house was transformed once again into a retail store for farm, milling and industry supplies.

The future of the opera house remains in question, but there are many who agree its history stuck around for more shows. Like the old Farmers Bank building, people claim to see lights on in the windows upstairs. Sometimes, the lights move from one room to the next, giving doubt to the idea that it was a simple reflection. Those who have gone in to investigate have found lights switched on, but they rarely see anyone who could have done it. Most of the stories from the opera house are tied to its music. The old performances are etched into the fabric of the building's reality, with the sounds of singing and shrill horns and strings trickling downstairs from the old theater. People have claimed to hear an entire audience breaking up with laughter, even though the floor has long been broken out from under what had been the seating. It seems the show will go on in the old opera house, no matter the state of the stage.

7

DEDICATED

THE KATE BARNARD SCHOOL

A stalwart landmark south of Tecumseh's downtown area commemorates one of Oklahoma's most remarkable—and, sadly, tragic—young leaders. Just as Kate Barnard would have wanted it, Barnard Elementary School is still in use today.

Catherine Barnard was born in 1875 in Nebraska; her mother, Rachel, passed away just two years later. Her father, John Barnard, struggled to get by and often moved to find work, leaving young Kate with family members until he could bring her to a new home. In 1891, Kate went to live with her father on his claim in what became Newalla, which was located right between the burgeoning towns of Oklahoma City and Shawnee. The younger Barnard worked as a teacher in one-room schools for a time, but she yearned for a broader reach to affect the territory. Her professional drive took her into clerical work for the government, which brought her to the World's Fair in St. Louis in 1904. There, she attended lectures about urban poverty that contained promising progressive ideas to alleviate the suffering that many people considered just a fact of life. Barnard grasped the ideas firmly and began campaigning for reform in her home state. In 1905, she lobbied the representatives at the Oklahoma Statehood Convention to outlaw child labor and create a commission that could oversee charities and prisons. Following Oklahoma's achievement of statehood, the Democratic Party endorsed her in the election to head the very commission that she had crusaded to build. Barnard, being a woman, could not vote for herself at the time, but she won the position by the widest margin of any race in Oklahoma's first election.

Modern structures have grown up around it, but the Barnard School remains resolute. *Provine photograph.*

As the first woman elected to a major state office, Barnard launched into her tasks, doing the work that is now performed by a number of different state departments. In addition to her regular duties of ensuring good treatment in facilities like orphanages and asylums, she campaigned for compulsory education, worked to change minds about child labor in a rural society and established a justice system for juveniles. In 1908, Barnard made headlines across the country by investigating contract prisons and creating new modes of rehabilitation through training. During Barnard's second term, however, her campaign to defend Native American orphans from abuse by those who seized their grants earned her powerful political enemies. Her department had its budget slashed again and again, and Barnard was driven into seclusion. She passed away in 1930.

It was during the height of Barnard's service to Oklahoma that Tecumseh needed a new school building. The old wood-frame building, which had served the town as a closer center of learning than the Friends' Church outside of Shawnee, had long been outgrown. A $15,000 bond built a new red-brick elementary school that was designed in the resolute Romanesque Revival style, with high peaks and bold arches over its doorways. In its application to the National Register of Historic Places, which was approved in 2000, it was said the Barnard School's design "connotes strength and stability and was most popular in institutional buildings such as schools." The school opened in October 1909, a date that stands out above the school's doors to this day. Barnard herself attended the dedication, which honored her for her efforts for the children of Oklahoma.

The school has eight classrooms, one for each grade to be housed in. To this day, children attend their studies in the same rooms that their ancestors sat in over a century ago. The National Register of Historic Places states, "The 1909 Barnard building is the oldest school building, in use or otherwise, that remains intact in Pottawatomie County." It is an entire generation older than several of the schools that were built by the Works Progress Administration (WPA) during the Great Depression.

Today, the upper floor of the school is closed up and used for storage, and many of the classrooms have been moved out to newer facilities that have been built around the campus; yet, there are still students who learn in the same rooms their great-grandparents learned in. Former students sometimes talk about how their classes in the basement always felt a little spooky, though few had any more reason to feel this way than it was simply a basement and they were kids. Others, however, say that they saw the phantom teacher walking the halls and rooms of the upper floors. The apparition is described as being a shorter lady who wears a long dress and has her head capped with a bulbous brown hairdo. She is rarely seen for long; she gives just a glimpse before the observer blinks and looks again to find that the room is empty. Interestingly, several people who have seen her claim that she was their own teacher from years ago, even though these witnesses never had the same teacher. This could be a case of mistaken identity, or perhaps it shows how many of the ladies who taught in the school followed the same style. Some believe that it may not be one single teacher; instead, they say it is the collective spirit of the school's many former educators. One further speculation about the phantom is that it is not actually any of the teachers from the school but is instead Kate Barnard herself checking in on her namesake school. She matched the figure's description, and one can be sure that not even death could slow her work to improve the lives of the youth of Oklahoma.

8

MURDERED BY HUMAN WOLVES

THE GRAVE OF KATHERINE CROSS

One of the most famous urban legends from Oklahoma stems from the Konawa gravestone that marks the final resting place of Katherine Cross. Born in 1899, Cross died in 1917, when she was, according to her gravestone, "murdered by human wolves." In 2004, Oklahoma writer Steven Wedel memorialized the story in his book *Murdered by Human Wolves*. The fictionalized retelling relates a horrific tale of werewolves in the early days of the state. During Wedel's research, however, the truth was revealed to be even more shocking.

Today, Cross rests in the Konawa Cemetery, which sits across the county line from the Violet Springs Cemetery. After Oklahoma achieved statehood, the whiskey town of Violet Springs dried up, and many people moved to Konawa. The wild saloon days were behind them, and the area settled into being a quiet farming community. It was years before the pace of everyday life was broken by Pretty Boy Floyd knocking over the First National Bank in 1931 and the WPA building a national guard armory that housed German prisoners of war (POWs). Yet, not everything was quiet. The front page of the *Shawnee Daily News-Herald* announced that the tragic death of a second young woman was caused by a "criminal operation" by Dr. A.H. Yates. There was no suggestion of skinwalkers or rougarou, however; the *Herald* stated, "Information placed in the hands of County Attorney Nichols led to a subsequent investigation, which, according to the county attorney, developed the fact that the girl would have become a mother within the next six months. Yates is accused of attempting to prevent that result." While the

Right: A rubbing shows the haunting words of Katherine Cross's grave. *Courtesy of Steven E. Wedel.*

Below: Even though her gravestone is gone, many pay their respects to Katherine Cross. *Provine photograph.*

century-old phrasing may not use the modern words, it is clear the medical procedure was an attempt to abort the pregnancy.

Cross was the second victim of Yates's medical mishandling. Elise Stone, who was also eighteen, had died two months earlier under similar circumstances—although Yates's medical statement said she died of "congestive chill." The townspeople demanded an investigation, and Stone was exhumed. As a protection from lynching, Dr. Yates was brought to Pottawatomie County and jailed there. Finally, Yates, along with his assistant, local teacher Fred O'Neal, was put on trial for first-degree murder. The testimonies were called an "awful story" in which no one wanted to disparage the girls' names, according to newspapers. Yates had even gotten permission from Cross's mother to perform the operation; she had told Yates "the girl was threatening to kill herself." The charges were lowered to first-degree manslaughter, and both Yates and O'Neal were later acquitted.

Blood ran hot enough that the Cross family had the engraver permanently state that Katherine was, in fact, murdered. Not only was her death a slaying, but it was work so savage, it was inhuman. She was laid to rest beside her grandmother Sarah Cross, who had died two years earlier at the age of seventy-nine. Eventually, the living Crosses moved southeastward to settle in Bennington. Dr. Yates died in 1931 and was buried across the cemetery from Katherine in a show of how small towns keep their complicated casts even after they pass on.

Thanks to the cryptic wording on Katherine's grave, her story does continue to be retold. Visitors leave stones and flowers on her grave as pilgrims to someone's resting place who was caught in extreme circumstances. This has also proven to be problematic, as the gravestone itself has been stolen multiple times. The first time, it was found ditched nearby; other times, it returned on its own. In July 2017, the gravestone disappeared, and as of 2020, it is still missing.

Wedel interviewed paranormal investigator Mary Franklin, who held an EVP session in the cemetery to try to uncover more details of Cross's life and death. At Yates's grave, she asked if werewolves did in fact live in Konawa; she said, "I got a one-word answer that is very plain: 'Several.'" If there are no literal shapeshifters, Oklahoma's history does contain people with a darker side.

9

Ghost Town

Romulus Cemetery

The term "ghost town" first appeared in the early twentieth century, when it was used to describe the trend of abandoned sites where people had once congregated. Its use is especially prominent in the American West, where towns sprang up as people rushed in to mine or try their hands at farming; once the opportunities vanished, so did the people. Oklahoma was unique, as its land rushes brought tens of thousands of people into the territory at once. Towns sprang up with them, but many soon faded, as there was no need for them when another post office or store was just a few miles up the way. Those towns that never hosted the railroad often had their populations move toward better economic prospects; they dwindled to little more than traces on outdated maps or cemeteries that bear their names.

The cemetery in Romulus, Oklahoma, is one such remnant of a ghost town, and it is well known for its paranormal activity. Romulus was established alongside its twin city, Remus, following the Land Run of 1891. With so many towns forming so quickly, there were often tricks to coming up with town names. Some named themselves after Native American heroes, such as Tecumseh; others picked up the names of local landowners, like Asher, which grew out of the estate of George Asher. Other towns had to be particularly creative, and several even chose matching names, such as Pink and the now-lost town of Brown, Oklahoma. Romulus paired itself with Remus, which was farther to the east, and they were each named for one of the twin brothers who are said to have been the founders of the

The cemetery of the ghost town Romulus, where residents are still heard saying, "Hello!" *Provine photograph.*

ancient city of Rome. While Romulus did outlast Remus, today its main street has lost its pavement. All that remains of the town is its Baptist church and cemetery.

Midway between Tecumseh and Asher, Highway 177 offers a quaint view of a seemingly quiet country cemetery that rests under the shade of tall cedars and oaks. It is a rich mix of history, with very old headstones and new ones of those who have recently passed. Gary Horcher, in his series "Oklahoma's Strangely Named Towns," states, "The pioneers of Romulus are still here, in a sense, with a story to tell." They do seem eager to share.

With its easy access just off the road and with substantial parking, the Romulus Cemetery is a favorite among paranormal investigators. Hobbyists and professional teams alike have spent countless nights among the gravestones, listening, watching and recording. Photographs taken at the cemetery frequently show controversial orbs and smudging that is said to be evidence of spirits making themselves known in front of the lens. Skeptics point out that these could be reflections of the flash or the results of a slow shutter on a dark night, but not all the images turn out this way, hinting that something more may be going on. Logan Corelli spoke of the time his team visited the cemetery; he said they witnessed shadows in the shape of people where no light source would have been casting them. To document this phenomenon, they took photographs, which showed the shadows even more vividly with the contrast in black-and-white. Someone—or something—was making its presence known.

More famous than images are the EVPs that are captured at the cemetery. A number of investigative teams have caught disembodied voices calling, "Hello!" or politely introducing themselves. Occurrences of spoken names have sent researchers rushing among the gravestones to see if the name correlates to any of the people who have been laid to rest; time and again, it does. Corelli's team also experienced EVPs, the vast majority of which he said were from female voices. Other sounds rang through the night, including nearby banging and ghostly whispers. They were alone in the cemetery—at least from a material perspective.

10

Watchful Spirits

St. Gregory's Abbey and University

After the devastating fire of 1901, the monks of Sacred Heart Mission rebuilt in southern Pottawatomie County, but their call soon led them elsewhere. The mission site, which was once the focal point of the region, was miles from the nearest rail line and was out of the way for modern students. It was clear that a new site would be better. At the same time, the community in Shawnee was looking for new ways to grow, and hosting Oklahoma's first Catholic college and new Baptist university seemed very promising. Shawnee donated the acreage and building funds that were needed to construct the five-story Benedictine Hall school building that was made of red brick with white trim and designed in the Tudor Gothic style that was popular on campuses around Oklahoma.

The school was originally called the Catholic University of Oklahoma, but everyone knew it as St. Gregory's after it was dedicated with St. Gregory the Great as its patron. In 1915, classes began, and the school served a wide range of students, from seventh grade to the collegiate senior year. With monks serving as educators, the entire Sacred Heart Abbey soon moved to the grounds in 1929, and it was also renamed under the patronage of St. Gregory. The school grew rapidly with the addition of new buildings, including the abbey church, with its stained-glass windows designed by Stephen Gyermek, in 1945 and the Mabee-Gerrer Museum of Art, which held the school's growing eclectic art collection. It also established a new cemetery, where oblates are buried; today, it serves as a thoughtful place of rest.

Above: Benedictine Hall stands as glamorous as it did over a century ago. *McCoy photograph.*

Right: Stained-glass windows commemorate St. Gregory the Great in the abbey church. *Provine photograph.*

The mission for the school changed over the years; it closed its high school in 1965 and later added a bachelor's degree program and a graduate studies program. As the belts of higher education tightened in the twenty-first century, the university closed. Its campus was bought by Hobby Lobby and was donated as an extension for nearby OBU, but the abbey remains at its heart, with today's monks still guiding the spirituality of Oklahomans in services at numerous churches.

With its decades of vibrant history, the campus has gained several rumored specters, and none is more famous than the Lady in White. Said to be the spirit of a student who took her own life after a bad breakup, the ghost is a classic mournful spirit. She is said to have appeared in several of the dorms, not only where she once lived; and she has been seen wandering around the campus as if she was lost. Doors have slammed on their own, and footsteps of heeled shoes have been heard ringing down halls at night. Several students have claimed they heard crying and even a young woman's voice, but they could never find anyone the sounds belonged to. Others have even claimed they saw her, a white, thin figure of a college girl who wept as she walked.

One St. Greg's graduate told the story of a prank gone wrong. To spook her suitemates, students from Vietnam who were especially sensitive to ghost

St. Gregory's Abbey carries on, shepherding the Oklahoma flock. *Provine photograph.*

The cemetery at St. Gregory's hosts a phantom figure of a monk who watches over the graves. *Provine photograph.*

stories, a girl had her friends dress her in a long white gown. She darkened her eyes and powdered her skin to appear brilliantly white. Wordlessly staring, she passed through the connecting doors and into the neighboring room. One suitemate went stone cold. The other tore out of the room, through the hall and down the stairs. They managed to stop her and confess the prank just after she had pushed through the dorm's doors and gone down the sidewalk. The storyteller imagined that if they hadn't caught her, she would have run all the way home to Oklahoma City.

Former teachers are also said to make appearances at the school. In the abbey's graveyard, a lone monk is seen standing vigil over his resting brothers. One former student who saw him said that she thought he was an old man there for a memorial visit. When she blinked, he was gone—faster than someone his age could have possibly moved. She decided not to move closer for a better look.

One monk is even more than a silent apparition; he tutors in the library. Late at night, students sometimes see a cheerful old monk strolling among the books, and some even speak to him before he vanishes. One story says that, as one student was struggling with his research, one of the brothers reached out to offer help. After suggesting books and even pointing out ideas for revision, the monk was gone. The student was grateful for the help and wanted more, so he hurried around the library asking if anyone had seen the monk. No one had any idea who he was talking about until someone recognized his detailed description. The monk was Brother William, a former English teacher who had passed away years before.

11

The Great Collector

Mabee-Gerrer Museum

We all like to hold onto a few special items, often showcasing them to others so that they may share in the experience that brought us so much emotion. Sometimes, collections also hold onto the ones who saved them.

Father Gregory Gerrer was born in a small French town in July 1867 under the name of Robert Francis Xavier Gerrer. In 1870 and 1871, the Franco-Prussian War broke out, prompting Father Gerrer's family to migrate to the United States. In 1891, he learned of the land run that was occurring in the Oklahoma Territory, and he soon made his way to the Guthrie area. In December 1891, he visited the community of Benedictine monks at the Sacred Heart Mission. The order proved inviting, so he entered the novitiate and took the name Gregory. In 1900, he became ordained in the priesthood and traveled to Rome to study art. He spent four years abroad before returning to the United States, where he began teaching at Sacred Heart and then at St. Gregory's after the Benedictine community moved to Shawnee. After leaving Oklahoma again—this time, from 1917 to 1932—Father Gerrer taught at the University of Notre Dame in Indiana and served as their curator during that time. He frequently returned to Oklahoma and even founded a museum that served as a space of inspiration on the prairie. After 1932, he returned to Shawnee and resumed his teaching duties at St. Gregory's, exciting others with the stories and relics from his travels. He would often sell or trade his paintings to help obtain anthropological objects or pieces of art for the museum. In 1931, he was inducted into the Oklahoma

The Mabee Foundation helped establish an expansive museum for Gerrer's collection. *Provine photograph.*

Hall of Fame for his work and dedication to the museum and studies of art. It is said that Father Gerrer would spend most of his days sitting in the museum, telling anyone who visited the history of his beloved objects. Father Gerrer passed away on August 24, 1946, but his collection lives on.

Located on the campus of St. Gregory's Abbey north of Shawnee, the Mabee-Gerrer Museum is one of the oldest museums in Oklahoma. Open since its founding by Father Gerrer over a century ago, this museum features a vast collection of art, artifacts and even a mummy or two. The idea of founding a museum came to Father Gerrer when he was on a pilgrimage to the holy land. While there, he was gifted with a small Egyptian scarab that had a hieroglyph of a goose on it. The friar took this gift as a sign that he needed to bring art and culture from around the world to Oklahoma.

The museum celebrated its centennial anniversary in 2019, but the building that currently houses the museum's artifacts is not the original location of the museum. The museum artifacts were first showcased in the rectory of St. Benedict's Church, where Gerrer was an assistant pastor. Later, the artifacts were moved into the art studio that he had built behind

Father Gregory Gerrer. *Provine photograph.*

the church. Gerrer's collection soon outgrew the space, and the artifacts were moved again. They later resided in the Benedictine Hall of the recently opened high school and college that were located at St. Gregory's. Expansions prompted the museum to hire Stephen Gyermek as the new curator in 1957. In 1962, the school was in dire need of more space for classrooms, so it was determined that the artifacts would be loaned out to the Kirkpatrick Science and Arts Foundation in Oklahoma City until a new building could be constructed in Shawnee. On April 7, 1979, sixty years after Gerrer's first opening, the new building was opened, thanks to the sponsorship of the Mabee Foundation.

Today, this museum holds an array of various artifacts and paintings from around the world. The walls are lined with art of all styles and sizes; it is showcased for all to see, as visitors are able to wander about the open floor plan of the building. The broad range of art gives people with just about every taste something to enjoy among the works from various artists through the decades. A stunning picture of a young woman from the Renaissance era may catch one's eye as she stares back longingly, making the viewer wonder what she was thinking as the artist seemed to capture her soul at that very moment in time. Or perhaps another may be more drawn to a carved ivory bust of a woman, with its intricate details so fine and precious that it appears she could turn and start talking at any moment. A full set of a knight's armor, chain link and all, stands ready to defend any young maiden whose honor may have been wronged. Other galleries show artifacts from the Far East, where samurai protect the empire from its neighboring enemies; others display ceremonial tribal masks from Africa and Native American beadwork. There are centuries' worth of antiquities that visitors can encounter thoughout the museum, but the most famous gallery shows artifacts from ancient Egypt.

Among the museum's priceless artifacts from around the world are the mummified remains of an ancient Egyptian known as Tutu, also known as Princess Menne. She died during the Ptolemaic Period, approximately around 332 BCE. Today, her mummified corpse, as well as her sarcophagus, appears in the museum's display. A second female mummy of poorer

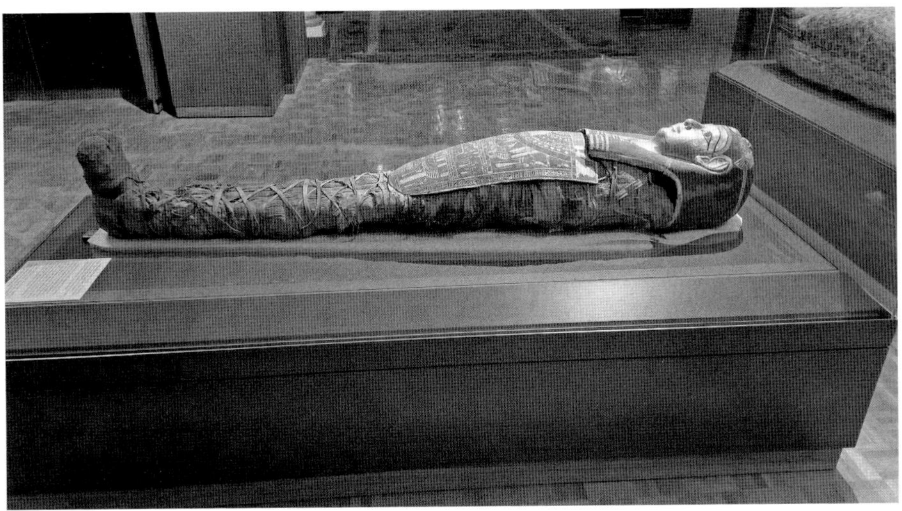

Princess Menne reclines in her gallery. *Provine photograph.*

stature that dates back to the second century CE is also featured in the exhibit, along with canopic jars and a mummified cat. These mummies were purchased by Father Gerrer in 1921, when another museum had undergone financial struggles; to this day, they are the only mummies permanently housed in Oklahoma.

Over the years, various reports have been made about hauntings at the museum. Again, the most famous report centers on the mummies. It is whispered among the visitors, especially the schoolchildren on fieldtrips, that the mummies rise from their cases and walk around the museum at night. This may be a little difficult, since they are kept under controlled-climate glass, but perhaps it is their spirits that choose to roam freely when the lights go down.

Another story takes place in the classroom and theater part of the museum, which was added around 1990. One woman shared her experience there; one night, while cleaning up around the stage area, she claims she saw a woman in white standing near the stage and even held a conversation with her. After a few minutes had passed, another group of people came in, and she saw the woman turn and float across the stage and up a set of stairs before disappearing. When the group asked if she was okay, she shared her experience with them. A young man in the group told her not to worry about it—that was just the ghost of the lady who often visits the theater and museum just to say, "Hello."

Another account occurred during the daytime hours as a small group of guests were visiting the museum. A man claimed to have been walking around the exhibit room alone when an older man approached him. The stranger asked how he was doing, and they continued to hold a conversation among themselves for several minutes. The man soon heard his wife and another guest approaching. As he turned toward them to introduce the stranger, he realized the man had disappeared. He described the man as being in his seventies or eighties and wearing an olive-grey archaeological outfit and hat, and he even claimed that he shook hands with him. The story ended when the man recognized the stranger again in the photographs of Father Gerrer that were taken before his death. One couldn't blame him for staying, really; after all, he had spent the better part of his life collecting his beloved objects and making them his life's work and passion. Why should death keep him from enjoying sharing them?

12
School Spirit
Jefferson Elementary School

Built in 1904, the old Jefferson Elementary School of Ward 6 was located on the corner of Kickapoo and Wallace Streets. It was a three-story square brick building with a large basement that covered the entire span of the building. An attic space was also noticeable in the historic photographs of the building. On March 28, 1924, a tornado struck Shawnee, and the Jefferson School took a direct hit as the tornado tore through the town. Principal Glenn Smith had dismissed school early that day, just before the storm arrived in town. He was named the hero of the day for likely saving the lives of several children, who would have died if they had remained at the school.

Despite the children being dismissed, the janitor, George W. Hill, did not leave the building. He later reported that he had not noticed the approaching storm and had been working in the fourth-grade room when the storm hit. He rushed to pull the door closed, but the winds were too strong. The wind pulled the doors from their hinges and tossed Hill back into the building, with the full force of the storm hammering down on him. He was able to free himself and found refuge by huddling in the southwest corner of the building. Most feared he was dead after seeing the devastation the tornado had caused to the building, but by great providence, he survived the ordeal with only a few minor injuries.

The tornado continued to wreak havoc throughout the town; it ultimately claimed the lives of nine residents and injured sixty-nine others. The ninth

The new Jefferson Elementary was built after the tornado of 1924 destroyed the first one. *McCoy photograph.*

victim was discovered a week later, when his discomposing body was found lying across his bed in his home. He had died from a head injury that he had sustained during the storm. As dark as the natural disaster was, Shawnee was again thankful that Jefferson Elementary reported no fatalities during the storm, despite the building being destroyed.

A new school building was rebuilt in the same location, but it did not open its doors until a decade later, in 1934. The building, designed by Hugh W. Brown, consisted of only one floor and was built using yellow brick. It is adorned with a beautiful frieze-style entryway on the front corner of the building. An auditorium was soon built, and in 1949, additions were constructed to accommodate the growing number of students. The offices and more classrooms were added in 1968. Today, the building still stands and continues functioning as a grade school.

Despite the fact that no deaths were reported at the school after the devastating tornado of 1924, the school is still rumored to experience paranormal activity. Doors open and close by themselves, toilets flush in unoccupied restrooms and disembodied footsteps seem to ring out down the empty school halls; this can all leave one feeling a little uneasy if they should find themselves alone in the building at night.

We have yet to find any evidence of a possible death at this location, but we do know that there have been deaths in the surrounding neighborhood—some during the time of the deadly tornado. Of course, not all spirits that haunt a location died there. Some may return to their homes, places they once knew or locations that brought them great happiness in life. Perhaps Glen Smith returned to his beloved school to keep a watchful eye over all the future children in his beloved home of Shawnee.

13

Afterlife in Luxury

Grisso Mansion

In 1926, the oil boom brought wealth to many Oklahomans, creating numerous millionaires overnight. One such millionaire was a man who went by the name of William Edward Grisso, but he was better known as Doc Grisso. Mr. Grisso was the local druggist, a country physician to the Seminole Tribe and the coroner, all of which earned him the nickname Doc. His legend and the home he built serve as some of the most captivating tales of the Shawnee area.

Located just southeast of Shawnee sits the town of Seminole, Oklahoma. Seminole was established in 1906 and was named after the Seminole Tribe that inherited the land after the Reconstruction Treaty. The Seminoles were originally located in Central Florida, but after the longest Indian war in history—the Seminole Wars, which lasted from 1835 to 1842—the tribe was forcefully removed and relocated to the Oklahoma Territory, in what is now Seminole County. More than three thousand Seminoles were forced to rebuild their lives in an unknown land, and they grew to become one of the five civilized tribes of Oklahoma.

Even in its early days, Oklahoma was no stranger to oil. Salt wells in the East had accidentally discovered black gold, and before Oklahoma achieved statehood in 1907, the Twin Territories, Oklahoma and Indian, produced more oil than any other state or territory in the country. The oil industry came to the Shawnee area almost by accident in 1923, when oilman Joe Cromwell's car broke down in Seminole. It was said that he liked the look of the land and decided to drill a test well. The No. 1 Bruner proved to be a gusher and led to the opening of the Cromwell Oil Field, hundreds of wells and millions of barrels of oil.

During the oil boom, the Seminole population exploded, bringing in thousands of new workers and residents overnight. The population of the town grew from 23,808 in 1920 to 79,621 in 1930. Seminole became the largest oil producer in Oklahoma in 1928, and it was producing 2.6 percent of the crude oil in the world. It was during this time that Mr. Grisso started obtaining mineral rights in the area. History usually portrays him as a great entrepreneur and businessman, but other unwritten tales portray him in a much darker light.

Stories passed down through some tribal members of the Seminole claim that Doc Grisso obtained the mineral rights though trickery and even forcible actions—some of which ended up in death. Rumor has it that he also had a common-law marriage with a young Seminole girl who went by the name of Suda Fixico Wesley. It was on Suda's four-hundred-acre allotment that the historic Grisso Mansion was built, though she did not live to see its construction completed. Within six months of the marriage, and after having his name added to the paperwork for her land and money, Suda died under mysterious circumstances. Many suspected she died of poisoning due to Mr. Grisso's chemistry background, but no investigation was ever launched into the mysterious death of the healthy fifteen-year-old girl. Soon after, Grisso married again and built a mansion for his new wife. The cost to build the mansion was around $750,000, which is equivalent to just over $11 million in today's market.

Grisso Mansion was built in 1928, in the Italian Renaissance style. It comprises twelve thousand square feet and contains twenty-six rooms, including eight fireplaces, multiple water fountains, a music room, a conservatory and a ballroom. Decorative tiles line the fountains and walls throughout the historic home, and hand-carved railings top the Spanish-style ironwork that leads up the staircases and around the walkways. Outside, guests find a centralized courtyard dividing the home, as was often seen in the Italian Renaissance style; it has a beautiful fountain that graces its center. Small rose ornaments can be seen throughout the home, as it was one of Mrs. Grisso's favorite designs; it is especially present in the master bedroom. The Grissos had fourteen servants, and most of them were members of the Seminole Tribe. Many of them worked there as indentured servants to pay off their debts that were owed to Doc Grisso from his druggist business.

Doc Grisso, his wife and his many servants may have moved on, but the history of the mansion continues to give visitors a glimpse into its long, mysterious past. Many rumors and stories are shared about the Grisso Mansion. Some of them are good—but others are not so good. Mrs. Grisso was considered a socialite who enjoyed the finer things in life, often hosting parties for groups of friends. Some stories take a darker turn, as rumors circulated about the rape of young Seminole women in the basement of the home during some of the parties. Could the energy that creates the hauntings that are witnessed today have been sparked during this time?

There are many ghost stories associated with the Grisso Mansion. For years, people have witnessed paranormal activity in and around the mansion. One story is that of a young Native girl who is often seen walking the grounds surrounding the home. Another is of a small Native boy who haunts the ballroom of the home; he has been seen by many eyewitnesses, including younger children, who describe him as being around six years old, and they say they saw him playing by himself. He has also been seen in various other locations around the home, including the basement. During one investigation, a paranormal team was able to obtain a voice saying the name "Kico," which is believed to be the young spirit's name. Interestingly enough, when the mansion was being built, they uncovered the skeleton of a young boy who was around the age of six; it was located in the area where the basement was built. Could the disturbance of the body have possibly caused the young man's spirit to remain in the home and roam the halls of the mansion? If so, he isn't alone.

Another spirit that has been witnessed at the mansion is that of a woman. She is often seen in one of the upstairs windows in the master bedroom, looking out over the driveway. Past residents of the home have reported coming home and seeing the woman standing there, staring into the distance. Many believe it is the spirit of Mrs. Grisso, still watching over her beautiful home that she loved so much when she was alive. There have also been reports of EVPs in which a woman's voice can be plainly heard answering questions or simply making comments.

The Seminole Nation purchased the mansion around 2012, and until 2019, it offered tours of the home. Reports were given over the years of paranormal activity in the home, including a lamp that would always turn itself on. It was also said that cupboards and doors would be opened by unseen hands, children giggling could sometimes be heard throughout the home and full-body apparitions and orbs were also witnessed around various locations in the home—many were captured in photographs. Could the dark hidden history of the Grisso Mansion be causing the spirits of the past to linger within its historic walls, or is it persistent energy from an era of oil-fueled luxury? Whatever the reason these spirits may linger, the fact is that they do, and they linger in and around the Grisso Mansion.

14

CHECKING IN

THE ALDRIDGE HOTEL

Originally named the Hilton Phillips Hotel, after its owner and oil tycoon Mr. Hilton Phillips, this ten-story architectural masterpiece has withstood the test of time as a prominent figure of the downtown Shawnee skyline. On August 10, 1927, Mr. Phillips approached the city with a proposal to erect a $400,000 structure in downtown Shawnee. A deal was struck between Mr. Phillips and the City of Shawnee that said the city would donate the land and Phillips would develop the grandest hotel in the area. The city called on the help of thirty residents, who donated time and money that was needed to purchase the land and present it to Mr. Phillips. In return, the chamber of commerce had a long-term lease on the building—ninety-nine years in exchange for $1. It wasn't a bad deal at all for Shawnee's first skyscraper.

On September 15, 1927, a groundbreaking ceremony marked the start of the construction of this historic site. Designed by the architect A.C. Davis and his son, the new hotel was to be fashioned after the grand Mayo Hotel in downtown Tulsa. It showcased a modern elevator, an open mezzanine on the second floor, marble floors and staircases, a restaurant and a ballroom located on the top floor. The hotel offered two hundred rooms, each with a view of the city. It also contained a governor's suite, a penthouse and multiple businesses in and around the building. By February 26, 1928, the hotel's doors were open for guests.

The penthouse became the home of Mr. Phillips. A self-made millionaire, Mr. Phillips was born in Maud, Oklahoma. He graduated from Maud High

The Aldridge still stands today, looking much like it did when Model As were common on the streets. *Courtesy of the Pottawatomie County Museum.*

School in 1920, then headed to Washington, D.C., where he served as a page for Congressman Tom D. McKeown in the House of Representatives. When he returned home, he took up an interest in the oil fields. He worked in purchasing for a major oil company until he opened his own office in Shawnee in 1925. His interest soon took him into politics, and he became the Democratic nominee for the state senate seat, but he was eventually beaten by Hoover in a landslide vote. In 1928, he was voted Shawnee's most valuable citizen, and he served in various organizations in Shawnee, including the Masonic lodge, the Elks Lodge and the American Legion. He was considered a very handsome man who was flamboyant and a high roller. Soon, he was looking beyond the Seminole oil fields and turned his interests to gold and silver in the Arizona, Colorado and Nevada regions. But his luck seemed to run out, along with the rest of the country, as the Great Depression began. He married Ruth Elizabeth Jones, a local beauty, in January 1929, only to end up divorced eleven months later. He was married again in 1933 to Juanita Allenbaugh, but that marriage was also short-lived and ended with divorce. By that time, he had lost his hotel; a downturn in oil prices prompted him to sell in November 1929 to the Aldridge Hotel Corporation. Phillips built a home in Nichols Hills, which is now part of Oklahoma City, where he soon suffered a six-month-long illness and two heart attacks. He eventually passed away at the young age of thirty-eight.

The Aldridge Hotel continued operating for years as a grand hotel, but it soon began regularly changing hands and often sat vacant. Still, it was a fixture of the city, and the Aldridge was placed in the National Register of Historic Places in June 2000. It was sold once more afterward, in December 2005; it was reopened as apartments for the elderly and disabled. Today, as visitors enter the majestic doors of the building, they are greeted by a large open lobby that is filled with beautiful pillars and white marble that lines the floors and staircases. A crystal chandelier adorns the center of the room, casting its glowing light around the spacious sitting area. To the right is a staircase that leads to the upper and lower floors, and the old front desk is where guests would have expected to be greeted by the concierge. The building gives visitors the feeling as if they have just taken a step back in time, and they become lost in the building's grandeur of yesteryear. Yet, underneath the beauty that abides in the building itself, there is something hidden deep within the building's past: stories of love lost, death and disaster.

The first story is that of a heartbroken bride. As she waited to walk down the aisle to her beloved fiancé, she learned that he was not coming to meet her. Devastated by his betrayal, she took her own life by hanging herself in the hotel. Her story does not end there, however. The spirit of the never-to-be bride is said to be stuck in her last moments, clinging to the desperation that had come over her. People claim to see a woman in white wandering the old halls of the hotel, still mourning the loss of her love.

Another story is that of a young girl who lost her life when she fell from the open mezzanine, which is located on the second-floor landing, to the marble floor below. She, too, is said to be a ghost that haunts the Aldridge. Many people report seeing a young girl running through the halls, and others have said they caught a glimpse of her before she quickly faded away.

The lobby of the Aldridge, which is still decadent today. *McCoy photograph.*

The second-floor space, which is no longer open, where a girl fell to her death years ago. *McCoy photograph.*

Management has closed off the open area on the second-floor building with a solid wood floor; it is now no longer open to the first-floor area.

Other ghost stories associated with the hotel are connected to a fire that was said to have broken out in the ballroom of the hotel. The facts about this possible occurrence are still unclear, as are the ghost stories, but there are those who claim they smelled smoke and heard shrieks, as if a party was coming to an abrupt end. The most recent ghost story attached to the hotel is associated with a stairwell that is located at the back of the building. The staff noticed what appeared to be orb activity in the stairwell and went to investigate. They used a voice recorder, and when they listened back to it, they heard what sounded like a man's voice saying, "Get out!" There have been other recorded deaths at the hotel as well. Some died of natural causes—others from self-inflicted wounds. Some people felt so hopeless and distraught that they decided to end their own lives by falling from the great heights of the Aldridge Hotel.

During an investigation of the location, Tanya and three other investigators were able to contact what they believed were some of the spirits that currently reside in this historic hotel. They were sitting in the ballroom area, conducting an EVP session, when Tanya suddenly felt a tightening in her chest. It proceeded to get worse. She felt as if someone had reached into her chest, grabbed her heart and started to slowly squeeze it. She thought to herself, "This is what it must feel like to have a heart attack." Tanya then started to experience pain running up and down the left side of her body, and she could feel a burning sensation on her left upper thigh. The discomfort and pain continued to intensify, and she had to excuse herself. The moment she left the area she was in, all the pain stopped. She went to the restroom to see if she had any injury on her leg. The area was clear, but there was a noticeable hot spot where Tanya had just felt the pain. After she had gotten up out of her chair, another investigator took pictures of where she had been sitting. The other investigator was able to obtain a picture of what appeared to be a white misty figure standing directly behind Tanya's chair.

Tanya wasn't the only one who had witnessed the chest pain. One of the other investigators who was sitting directly to her left also started feeling a similar pain. A third investigator reported feeling the pain in his left side as well. They had all been sitting in a very close circle. They did have one piece of equipment respond while they were investigating the area; Tanya had placed a parascope (a piece of equipment that lights up when it comes into contact with a possible spirit) near the entrance of the restrooms, and it responded not long after their investigation began. The group's ghost radio also provided them with various names, as well as some other possible clues that may help them discover some of the identities of the spirits that continue to reside at the Aldridge Hotel. The group moved on to their next location, the basement. As they were heading down, Tanya asked the staff if someone had passed away from a possible heart attack in the lobby. She received confirmation that there was a history of such a death that had occurred there. Could the spirit that affected so many of them have been letting them know that it was still around?

With the group's time being limited, they decided to stay in one small room in the basement area to conduct their investigation. The room contained various items, including an oil painting of Mr. and Mrs. Aldridge, which was placed neatly against the wall. They didn't have to wait long for activity to start occurring. The basement had a heavy feeling, and one of the group's members, Keisha, reported feeling a creepy, chilling feeling once they turned the lights off. The group placed a K2 (a mel meter device that detects changes in EMF levels) in front of the portrait, and they placed another EMF device in the middle of the room. They also placed a few other investigating tools (parascopes, temperature devices and motion sensors) around the room and started recording on the audio devices. After a few quick hits on the ghost meter, their ghost radios started responding. At first, the responses seemed very typical, and they believed the spirit they were talking to was that of a child. Then, things began to change.

A dark feeling of unrest came over the team. One team member started to become affected by whatever entity was trying to communicate with them. She reported feeling an emotional change and started to experience feelings that she knew were not her own. She stated she felt like she had a permanent state of chills, something she simply could not shake. Soon after, their ghost radio began saying some negative things: "Let me out," "Leave me" and more. "Psychopath," "insanity" and "go away" followed. "Bones" and "crawling" also came through, and at one point, the team audibly heard a disembodied growl directly behind them.

With the investigation time ending, they gathered their equipment and returned to the car. Despite leaving the building, Keisha was unable to shake the feelings that she had started experiencing. Another team member, Chris, who is also Tanya's case manager and a light worker, joined the team off location. Keisha reported having strange feelings come over her with the arrival of Chris—feelings she had never experienced before. She felt inexplicably fearful and wary. The group said prayers, and the dark heavy feelings that Keisha had experienced began to be relieved.

Once outside the hotel, the team realized that the area they had been sitting in was right next to the old abandoned hospital. It was then that they realized they must have been witnessing a transient spirit from next door. With what they had already collected, and after reviewing further evidence, they believe that one of the spirits they encountered is attached to the old hospital and that they possibly had a psychiatric disorder. This spirit was drawn to their location while they were conducting the investigation; this can occur—and often does—when a spirit feels someone is able to feel them or communicate with them, especially if they are within close proximity of where an investigation is being held. The group is unsure why the spirit decided to attach itself to Keisha or why fate took over and made sure their light worker was able to join them to send the attachment away, but as paranormal investigators, they are aware that these things can happen, and they try to be prepared to deal with them when they do.

With the investigation over and Keisha back to her regular loving self, the group knew they had left the Aldridge exactly as it was when they entered its majestic doors—beautiful, haunted and filled with the memories of all the years gone by.

15

A Modern Ruin

Harjo School

Just fifteen miles southeast of Shawnee, off Highway 9A, there sits an area known as Harjo. The post office at Harjo was established on June 24, 1921, only to be discontinued on August 3, 1954. Now considered a ghost town, this small community once boasted an award-winning sports team, the Harjo Hornets. Long past are those glory days, as the Hornets' old school sits empty and in disrepair, a mere shadow of what it once was.

Located in a small wooded area, set back from the highway at the end of a long, dusty Oklahoma road, the small schoolhouse sits, void of any life. The windows are only shattered glass, and various parts of the roof have caved in. The building is a dangerous location for any would-be ghost hunter who tries to trespass onto the property, which should never be attempted. Better known as Harjo Consolidated District No. 5, the school was built as a united location for several smaller schools. Built around 1930, the school consisted of eight classrooms, a cafeteria, an auditorium with a stage, restrooms and a gymnasium. A residential house was also built on the school's grounds to house the acting principal of the school. Harjo, which means "brave beyond description" in the Creek language, is located on what was originally Seminole land; it was allotted to them by the government prior to statehood. Nearby is the Rose-Fast Site, a prehistoric Native basecamp that dates back to the Woodland Period (around 1000 CE). Since the land the school ruins sit on has such a long and vast history, it is no wonder that stories of the paranormal linger around the decaying walls of this old school.

The remains of Harjo School sit abandoned on a lonely lot. *McCoy photograph.*

Kale Epperson, along with a team of investigators, first studied the building in 2012. From the minute they pulled onto the property, they said they felt as if they were being watched from every direction. One of members on the team, a Native American person, said it felt as if the spirits did not want them there. Still, they continued. Once the equipment was unloaded and the team was set to go, they entered the building just outside the old cafeteria. One investigator stated that they saw a figure of a young Native American person standing in the doorway of the cafeteria. The juvenile appeared to be wearing a white shirt and pants. No footsteps were heard approaching or leaving the area, and upon investigation, there were no disturbances of the surrounding debris—no earthly soul had been seen.

From there, the team moved on to the main school building. The interior walls were painted in bold colors, and they lined either side of the hall, stretching far back into the school. Exposure to the elements had made it possible for the outside vegetation to stretch long vines along the small corridors of the old building. Various walls in the building had been decorated with murals of landscapes, and they could still be seen. Mold spotted the walls, adding one more deadly element to the mix of danger that one may expect when entering a building that is in such a state of disrepair. With old ceiling tiles, wiring, metal and wood looming above their heads, the team was cautious as they pushed farther into the belly of the building.

As the team members positioned themselves along the hallway, they started an EVP session. During the session, several team members witnessed what appeared to be shadow figures peeking around the doorways of the classrooms down the hall. As the night continued, the team periodically saw what appeared to be human-shaped masses moving from classroom to classroom. They asked the spirits if they could make a noise to allow them to know that they were with them. Almost immediately, a large crashing sound came from the auditorium. The investigators entered the hallway to head toward the auditorium, and something flew by, as if it had been thrown at them. They looked for the object, but due to all the debris on the floor, it was impossible to tell just what had been thrown. As they started walking through the auditorium, Kale noticed a Native American male in full cultural attire walk across the hall and enter the auditorium seating area. The group rushed over to the area only to find that the spirit had disappeared. They decided to set up another EVP session in the auditorium to see if they could communicate with the spirit they had just seen. Then, the paranormal activity escalated.

The room began to feel heavy, and a general sense of unwelcomeness began to take over the team. The group started to notice that things were being thrown at them from unseen hands once again. One object that was thrown was a small piece of sharp glass, which did hit one of the investigators on the scene. Kale soon realized that the only members of their team who seemed to be getting targeted were the White ones. Once again, Kale noticed the Native American man standing at the back of the room. He appeared to be looking toward the group with an angry expression. Once Kale informed the team that he felt the spirit was targeting certain members of their group, a large crash was heard once again; this time, it came from behind the stage area. Kale informed the other investigators that they should leave the area due to safety concerns. He and the other Native American investigator stayed behind to investigate the possible cause of the loud noise they had just heard.

Kale claimed that once the other team members left the area, the air felt lighter, and glass was no longer being thrown. Behind stage, they discovered a large piece of debris lying on the floor. They decided to end the investigation that night for fear of continued hostility from the spirits. Later, while reviewing their recordings, the team noticed that they had successfully obtained several EVPs, each stating clearly "Get out" and "Leave." The team also obtained an EVP of what appeared to be an unknown (to them) Native American language being spoken.

Could the spirits that haunt the school be the restless spirits of a Native American tribe, unhappy with the White settlers who had pushed their way into their homelands? Or, are they simply the restless spirits from more recent past that still linger in the halls of their old school? As time passes, Mother Nature continues to take hold of the old schoolhouse, reclaiming the land as her own. Soon, nothing but the memories of the land may remain.

16

Crossing Over

Bridges of Pottawatomie County

The flow of water carries powerful energy. It can be felt by the peace that settles over you when you stand still and let a current roll around your form or sit nearby and listen to its splashing. Folklore says this energy flows into the spiritual realm as well, loosening the veil between it and the physical world. Roads, too, carry an energy from the many people who have traversed it. Bridges, where those roads and waterways meet, hold a special mix of those powers. Famous "cry baby" bridges dot the Oklahoma landscape, each with its own version of a story of an infant and, often, its mother passing away nearby, even though its spirit continues on through the energy of the water. The area south of Shawnee offers an array of stories linked to several of its bridges.

Fortson said that the first bridge in the eastern part of the county was built by farmer H. Barrett and his neighbors. "First thing...after they had thrown up shelter on their quarter sections was to get a road through to the county seat." He said they began "chunking rocks into the low places and dragging trees out with their oxen" to bridge Brier Creek. It was all for profit; they wanted to be able to haul their cotton as soon as the crop came in (which did well, with over 2,800 pounds from little cultivation of the virgin ground).

Just a couple of miles up Little River from where that first bridge spanned it is a section of Brangus Road that meets E1250 Road. The dual bridges there make up what legends in that part of the county have called for generations a "Ghost Bridge." Chief J.R. Kidney of the Tecumseh Police Department, a native and longtime resident, said that it was "a destination for high school kids for years." Rural teenagers who needed somewhere to go would hang out there, and they made Ghost Bridge a popular spot for nighttime jaunts. Kidney mentioned he had been out there several times with groups of people and had never seen anything. "When you're alone, though," Kidney said, "there's a feeling that you're being watched." He continued by saying that people claimed to feel a presence there with them, as if someone was peeking over their shoulder. Despite getting that feeling of a person behind them, turning around proved that they were standing there alone. Other storytellers add that, if you are willing to stand still near the bridges on a quiet day, the sounds of screams can be heard trickling out from underneath. Skeptics say that it is a trick of the wind blowing, but believers hold that these screams can be heard on windless days—and especially at night.

Various origins of the story can be traced back to the wild days of bootlegging in the county or, even earlier, to a Native American ambush. The legend has evolved over the past generation; its name has been changed to "Ghost Boy Bridge," and it is said that a kid died there. Chief Kidney recalled, "Shorty Drake jumped off the bridge sometime in the 1970s or 1980s." Kidney said Drake did not, in fact, die in the fall; he was only injured. "He was paralyzed after the fall. Still, some people said that he'd died, but he didn't." The more nail-biting version of the story seemed to catch on, and today, youngsters head out to see if they might hear a cry from Ghost Boy Bridge.

People who go backroading say that Ghost Boy Bridge is just the first in a long trail of local sights. Continuing south on Brangus Road will take adventurers down the steep slope of Thrill Hill and then to Dead Man's Curve, where the road turns after crossing Sand Creek. The bridge there offers its own legend of a woman drowning her children to protect them from worse fates at the hands of marauders.

For those from the far southern part of the county, "Ghost Bridge" is the name used to describe the Wanette-Byars Bridge, which spans the Canadian River. Built in 1902 as part of the Eastern Oklahoma Railway, it carried trains for nearly forty years until it was converted to a road for cars and trucks. Even before that, it was a pedestrian walkway for those who did not want to risk fording the river, which was treacherous, with quicksand and fallen trees hidden in the murky water. The bridge, with its three spans, each said to be the longest in the state, withstood tremendous floods and 160-ton locomotives. Vandals struck in 1992, torching its wooden deck with a diesel-driven fire so hot that it warped the riveted

"Ghost Bridge" has become "Ghost Boy Bridge" to younger generations, as the urban legend has evolved. *Provine photograph.*

One of the bridges on Brangus Road, where cries from spirits long past can be heard. *Provine photograph.*

steel beams. But not even that could destroy the bridge, which reopened and relieved drivers of a twenty-eight-mile detour when trying to cross the river. It was on this bridge that Old Man Wilson was gunned down in a fight over a hunting dog. Folks say that Wilson may still be seen walking across the bridge, rifle in hand. Others claim to hear phantom shouts and even gunfire as the violent event replays itself. Wilson's last moments prove as eternal as the bridge itself, tempting legend-trippers to keep a careful watch as the Canadian River drifts by underneath.

17

UNIDENTIFIED

THE STRANGER THINGS SEEN AROUND SHAWNEE

More than ghosts haunt the area around Shawnee. Creatures that defy traditional scientific explanation echo in the legends that existed in the region long before the land run. Researcher Jim Whitehead has long collected and studied the stories of these sightings, and Pottawatomie County offers up fascinating cases. Many of the stories tell of creatures that bear a strong resemblance to one another.

Whitehead related a story from outside of Pink of people who were driving down a rural road when they saw a beast step out in front of them from the tree line. They described it as a "troll" that walked on its hind legs. It was covered in shaggy black hair, and it had a potbelly that stuck out in front of it. There have been numerous reported cases of bigfoot sightings; the elusive creature is said to be a North American primate. While perhaps the most famous bigfoot sightings have occurred in the Pacific Northwest, Oklahoma is no stranger to bigfoot. The dense forests of the southeastern part of the state offer numerous films from famous encounters, such as the siege of Honobia in 2000, and the bigfoots' reach goes well into the Cross Timbers.

Time and again, people have been hiking, checking cattle or even at home when they spotted a tall, hairy creature walking on its back legs. Whitehead stated that one case in Pottawatomie County even reported a white bigfoot with ivory-colored hair. One Oklahoma man caught a glimpse of what he called "a humanoid tiger." His security light flicked on, showing his yard that ran up to the woods. In the light was a creature that stood tall on its hind legs; it was about the height of a fully grown man. Its body was covered in orange fur with some brown striping on it. As soon as it realized it was being watched in a spotlight, the creature took off back into the woods. Another story came from a coworker of a woman who said she was being stalked by a dogman. These beasts are said to be large canids that walk upright with long arms and dark, shaggy fur. She would take Moccasin Trail on the north edge of the county to and from work, and several times on the journey, she saw what she described as a "werewolf" sitting in the grass by the road, its long limbs outstretched, watching her drive by. It became so terrifying that she began leaving early to take the long way around, avoiding the road altogether.

While most of the creatures are only seen, one man shared his story of being attacked by one of them. As he was driving on a country road, a beast that stood over six feet tall burst out of the woods and slammed into his truck. He said it purposefully rammed him and continued to pound against the side and rear of the truck until he managed to escape at high speed. It was the Deer Woman, he said; he recognized it as a body covered by deer hair.

Whitehead believes many of these stories are talking about the same strange animal. "The details all line up," he said. "It's all in how you interpret them." He suggested that different cultural backgrounds give people different views of what they suddenly see. People of English descent talk about trolls and apes, while those of German backgrounds recognize dog-like features from werewolf legends. The man who wrote about being attacked by Deer Woman was Native American. These varying stories may be the results of seeing a similar thing in different ways.

Whether the creatures in the indomitable Cross Timbers woods are of the same breed or not, there are plenty of witnesses of "Big Ben," the giant turtle of Twin Lakes. The Twin Lakes Reservoir started as one lake in 1935, when the WPA worked to create water conservation and flood-control programs. The second lake was added in 1960, and the two were connected with a canal to make a total surface area of 2,400 acres. The story among fishermen says that, years ago, when the first dam was built, they began feeding a remarkably large turtle that would swim fearlessly up to their boats. Through the years, they kept feeding Big Ben, and as they did, he grew to truly gigantic proportions—some estimate his shell to be some three feet across. Some say that he is a red-eye slider of aberrant size, but others agree that Big Ben is an alligator snapping turtle. Scientifically, those dinosaur-like turtles in aquariums have been seen to grow to Big Ben's estimated size and weigh upward of 200 pounds. A story in Kansas tells of an alligator snapping turtle that was caught in 1937 that weighed in at 403 pounds. With the fishermen on his side and estimates that alligator snapping turtles can live for up to two hundred years in the wild, Big Ben may just beat the Kansas record.

In addition to creatures in the woods and lakes of Pottawatomie County, strange lights appear in the sky. During a 2014 broadcast of the station's 6:00 a.m. morning show, KOCO 5 showed a live view of the phenomenon from the mounted camera above Grand Casino. A rectangular white object streaked over the I-40 traffic, heading for the ground nearby. Shortly thereafter, the news team posted the video as a clip of a UFO in the literal sense of the word: it was an unidentified flying object. They prompted viewers to offer their suggestions. Speculations came in, labeling the object a drone, a gliding bird and a small meteor. Others suggested it was swamp gas or weather balloons. Many said that it was an insect illuminated by the reflected light of the camera. UFO believers pointed out how quickly the object seemed to move (it was estimated to be moving at one thousand miles per hour by one comment) and noted that the recent CERN Large Hadron Collider reactivation had been scrubbed along with a spike in world UFO activity.

KOCO investigated further by contacting Steve Carano and Steven Fowler, professors at Rose State College. Rebutting the ideas that it was a reflection, the men pointed out how the image is very clear and shows no typical diffusion. They determined that it was likely a meteorite "the size of less than a pea or even smaller" based on its very straight trajectory and high speed. Most likely, it did not even reach the ground before it finished burning up.

Since this light was a probable visitor from space—albeit a small rock—many believe that more intelligent life inhabits the Oklahoma skies. One woman shared a story of being in her backyard with friends late one night in the eastern part of the county when she saw a light trailing up above them. It was too slow to be a shooting star, so at first, she thought it was a plane. Then, it stopped and hung in the air. She called to her friends, who were also watching the light. While they watched, another plane-like light came up to it and stopped. A line extended out from it to the first light, and then, they both moved on together as if the second were towing the first. No one was sure what they saw, except that it was very much unidentified.

18

The Show Goes On

Ritz Theater

For over a century, 10 West Main Street has been a center of entertainment for the Shawnee community. One proprietor, Leo Montgomery, has always kept an attentive eye over the theater—for more than fifty years before his death and for more than fifty years after.

The building boomed alongside the town with the coming of the railroad; it had been opened as a dry goods store before it evolved into a boardinghouse with shops downstairs. It soon evolved again, as the rapidly growing town needed more proper entertainment; this led to the opening of the Cozy Theater in 1911. Shawnee was home to over twelve thousand people by then, and the Cozy Theater was the premier spot of the vaudeville circuit in the region. Actors, singers, dancers and comedians flowed steadily into town, where audiences were hungry to see something new in the days before radio and television. In addition to the typical fare, managers would often bring in special animal acts, lectures and, especially, moving picture shows.

In 1914, Jake Jones Sr. purchased the Cozy Theater as the start of a cinema theater empire that would last generations. Jones, who had been born in Lebanon in 1888, came to America to take advantage of the land of opportunity. He had tried his hand at several ventures, including a running candy store, before he settled on the Cozy Theater and its adjoining boardinghouse. Jones's speculation into theaters proved to be a fortunate move, especially in 1926, when major renovations turned

The Ritz Theater continues to be a heart of entertainment for Main Street. *Provine photograph.*

the theater into the first cinema in Shawnee, equipped to show the newfangled "talkies" that linked film and sound. The overhaul included a new name for the theater, which highlighted its place on the pinnacle of glamour: the Ritz. The Shawnee Fire Department came out to the theater shortly after it opened to show off its engine and help promote the film *The Fire Brigade*. When *The Towering Inferno* premiered in 1975, the fire department came out again; this time, they came with a state-of-the-art snorkel truck, which had a hydraulic, multi-directional ladder and an affixed spray cannon. By this time, the Ritz had been updated to its modern façade and elaborate marquee, which had been taken from the closed Bison Theater.

Jones Sr. rapidly expanded with more theaters like the Criterion, which was built in 1927, and the State, which was renamed in 1935. Future Joneses went on to open drive-ins and other theaters, and they donated the Ritz to the Society for Revitalization of Downtown Shawnee in 2000. Through hard work and community outreach, the Ritz has returned to its vaudeville roots, with live performances ranging from concerts and comedians to community theater. In the recent remodels, the theater has moved away from cinema; much of the auditorium itself has changed, yet the Ritz still holds onto its charm from yesteryear. The smooth curves and bold eagle of its Federalist Revival style—a precursor to Art Deco—create eye-catching architecture for Main Street. The expanded double marquee from the Bison harkens back to the days of monster movies and double features. Inside, the lobby boasts a checkered-tile floor and wide counters that have presented candy to generations of theatergoers.

The legends of the Ritz Theater are rich with ghost stories. People tell of lingering spirits from the building's days as a boardinghouse, including a young lady who passed on from pneumonia. Other stories say that residual energies from the building's many theatrical performances will replay themselves, with music and singing from performers long dead filling the auditorium. Whole conversations with different voices will crop up among the empty seats. Most of the stories, however, center on Shawnee personality Leo Montgomery.

Montgomery spent nearly his entire life in the theater. He grew up in one of the apartments upstairs, and when his elders passed on, he continued living in the building. Montgomery's father had managed the theater for a brief time after it opened, and young Leo took over in the 1910s. He performed all the necessary tasks, from booking and lighting to cleaning and selling tickets, when they needed to be done. When the Ritz was reborn as a movie house, Montgomery added "projectionist" to his repertoire. It was his title for the next thirty-nine years.

Reportedly, however, Leo Montgomery didn't even like movies; that was just his job. He would set up the projector and sit back to read in his easy chair in the projection room while the people in the theater below enjoyed the show. To ensure he never missed a beat, Montgomery invented a mirror system that gave him perfect views without having to get up from his chair, and they alerted him as to when he needed to ready the projector to switch reels. Montgomery never retired from his work. In 1965, he suffered a heart attack during a show and quietly passed alone in the projection booth. No one knew he was gone until the film reel ran out, showing a blank screen, and the audience went to investigate.

Even after his death, Montgomery still watches over the theater. It has notorious issues with its lights. A flickering bulb may be a simple electrical issue, even with the newly installed wiring, but Montgomery's unseen hand flips entire switches on and off. He is even said to make appearances as a face looking out from the projection booth and an entire phantom walking the aisles in clothes that were fashionable decades ago. With such vivid activity, several groups of paranormal investigators have been drawn to the Ritz. None have faced any threats, but some have captured images in photographs and voices in EVPs that show someone is there, watching them.

19

HIDDEN

THE HISTORIC BISON THEATER

Sitting on the corner of Philadelphia and Main Streets is a three-story cream-colored building that was once known as the Bison Theater. Originally built by Griffin Theaters and opened in October 1927, the theater later became one of the Video Independent Theaters of Oklahoma City. It remained open until the mid-1950s, when it closed its doors forever on the cinema life it once knew. Yet, something unseen remains there today.

The Bison was grand in its heyday. It only contained one large screen, unlike today's multi-screen cinemas, but it held seating for up to 1,080 patrons. The stage offered a space for live performances from traveling shows and screening films. Guests were greeted by the twinkling lights of the marquee, the larger-than-life actors' names and the faces of the golden age of Hollywood who beckoned them to enter the doors, walk the red carpet and enjoy a night at the cinema. The Bison's acoustics offered an experience that most other theaters did not at that time. A large dome ceiling topped the theater, creating a natural surround-sound effect. The ceiling of the dome twinkled like the stars in the night sky, adding to the artistic effect of the theater experience for its patrons.

With the introduction of the Hornbeck Theater, the Bison soon took a backseat and ended up being the "second-run movies" theater. With more and more families being able to purchase televisions for their private homes, the movie business started to slowly decline, causing the older theater to close its doors. In 1966, the building's exterior underwent major renovations, as did some of its interior. Walls were added, and the original theater's seating

The façade of the Bison Theater represents an era of luxury that is rarely seen in today's cinema. *Courtesy of the Pottawatomie County Museum.*

area was closed off to the public. The windows of the second and third floors on the front of the building were covered, no longer visible from the street. The V-shaped marquee was removed and reinstalled a few blocks down on the front of the Ritz Theater.

Several new businesses graced the once-grand Bison's building. Functioning as a western wear store, a church and a few other enterprises along the way, the building went through numerous changes over the years. In the 1970s, there was even a bar known as the Cave located in the basement area. Sometimes, there were long periods that the building sat empty, and it is currently vacant today. The latest business that was known to be in this location was the Old Wishing Well Antiques, and when it was there, paranormal activity started being reported.

Employees of the antique store started to notice strange things occurring not long after the store moved into the historic location. They reported that they often saw what appeared to be a male apparition wandering around the shop area and leaning over the balcony of the old theater. One female employee reported feeling a touch of an unseen hand as it caressed her cheek. A local paranormal team was called in to investigate the property to see what or who might possibly be haunting the old theater building. Lisa Lawrence Ghariani and her all-girl team took on the task of investigating the paranormal activity.

Lisa stated that most of the activity they witnessed and recorded were EVPs. She recalled that one EVP they obtained while under the dome of the old theater was a man's voice saying "darlin'" in a southern accent. The EVP was a Class A recording, meaning it was very clear and could easily be made out. Since her team is an all-female group, there were no men present during the investigation, making the voice stand out even more. Other EVPs were recorded downstairs in the shop area. The team also witnessed several orb anomalies throughout the building—one of which was featured on the Channel 9 news. The team returned on multiple occasions to investigate the building, and they conducted group ghost tours there for a time, showcasing the spooky side of downtown Shawnee for curious guests.

A few additional paranormal teams have also investigated the location, and each witnessed their own paranormal activity, including disembodied footsteps, disembodied voices, knocking sounds from outside the windows and full-body apparitions. One apparition was of two men fighting, and the fight ended with one man's death. Rumors have circulated that a murder took place in the building sometime in the 1930s, making some wonder if it is perhaps the restless spirit of the victim who continues to haunt the walls of the old theater, unable to find peace in the afterlife.

20

Signs from the Other Side

Hamburger King

The past literally lives on at Hamburger King, the hopping Shawnee eatery that harkens back to the bygone era of lunch counters. Out-of-towners travel for miles to take in its tasty fare, which hasn't changed since their grandparents ordered it years ago for five cents. To place an order, diners pick up their table's phone along the wall and call in, a tradition that is rarely seen today outside of old films and sometimes needs explaining to youngsters.

Mansour George Macsas, who emigrated from Lebanon, began the original Hamburger King in Bristow, Oklahoma, in 1922. The restaurant worked out so well that he invited his brother, Joseph, to follow suit with another Hamburger King in Shawnee. These were the early days of chain restaurants, a whole generation ahead of today's giants like McDonald's, and only companies like A&W and White Castle followed a similar experiment. Hamburger Kings thrived across Oklahoma for years, and today, the Shawnee Hamburger King is still going strong, proclaiming, "Famous for hamburgers since 1927." In addition to the burgers, Hamburger King offers a menu straight from Oklahoma's palate, with catfish, hamburger steak, cornbread and potatoes with gravy, as well as its award-winning "300 Block" Chili, reflecting the longtime residency of the restaurant on Shawnee's Main Street.

According to Cindy Hardin and Colleen Macsas, the third-generation proprietors of Hamburger King, the building itself dates back to Oklahoma's achievement of statehood. For a long time, it was home to Burt's Furniture, and the upstairs storage area still holds some of the large pieces that were

The Hamburger King has been a familiar sight for Shawnee eyes for nearly a century. *Provine photograph.*

Even when empty, the Hamburger King stays active with the sounds of footsteps and moving furniture. *Provine photograph.*

passed down through the years. The descendants are still running things today as a family affair; it's now on its fourth generation of servers, and they agree that the spirits of the old-timers still dwell there.

People typically think of hauntings when they hear footsteps and furniture moving in an empty building at night. At Hamburger King, the footsteps are said to sound at all times of the day. It is hardly noticeable when crowds are there, but when employees are opening early in the morning or doing the accounting at night, leather-soled footfalls ring out from the empty rooms. Once, a worker who was opening alone became so scared of hearing the sounds and being unable to find the culprit that she ended up stacking five-gallon bags of cola syrup against the office door to barricade herself in while she called the police.

There are also plenty of other sounds, like the thumping and clinking bowls. Hardin said, "Ninety percent of that was an old ice maker....You have to learn what the sounds of the machines are." Yet, there are times when the sounds are clearly something else. Macsas once described carefully going through the kitchen and switching off each machine, one by one, then still hearing the thrumming of someone there with her. More sounds come from upstairs, which witnesses describe as someone "moving furniture."

After going up the only stairs, they find the storage room empty, perhaps just echoing the days of Burt's. At one point in the late winter, the activity became especially raucous. After some thought, the Macsases decided that it was their father, William. "We had closed one whole week for the state fair and then, since Christmas was a Wednesday, we went ahead and closed that Monday, too. This is probably him saying, 'You closed too many days. You need to stay open for your customers…and to make money!'"

Some may fear the seemingly inexplicable signs of the supernatural touching the natural world, but Hardin and Macsas take it all in stride. Macsas stated that a piece of land behind her house was once the site of a massacre, and even today, there is still a sensation of sadness and being watched present on the property. The land itself is very pretty, with a creek and wooded area, but there is still that oppressive feeling. Once, she even saw a figure dressed in white walk past her kitchen window from the spot. When she ran out to check who it could be, the figure was nowhere to be found. Hardin and Macsas recalled seeing omens before the death of a loved one, such as a dog howling underneath a window or an owl flying during the daytime. The biggest sign was a complete rainbow with its end touching the ground, which is said to show that there is beauty, even at an ending. Hardin said, "My personal take on that is it's God saying, 'I got this.'"

21
THE LAST CHANCE SALOON
OLD AT&SF PASSENGER STATION

A boarded-up, two-story building sits just west of the tracks on East Main Street. This historic building is wasting away with the passing of time, but it was once a building that was loved—it is now being forgotten. On the back wall of the building is a mural that states, "Santa Fe Trading Post," a witness to the time when passenger trains traveled these tracks, bringing people from far and wide to visit the booming town of Shawnee. Once known as the AT&SF Passenger Station, this building, like many others along the historic downtown streets of Shawnee, played host to an array of businesses over the next century.

"J.H. Wellington" can be seen stamped around the front doors of the building, alongside the year it was built, 1902. Like many buildings around town, this one has seen its good and bad times—some leaving an everlasting mark within its broken-down walls. The upstairs, like most businesses in the old district, contained living quarters or rooms for rent. This was an easy way for the owners to make a quick buck and maximize the use of their property to help increase their financial situation. With it being right beside one of the major train depots, it was a prime spot for any weary travelers who needed a place to rest their heads.

Not much is known about the building in historic documents, but some people do possess tidbits of history about this remarkable location. Lisa Lawrence Ghariani was lucky enough to investigate the location with her team many years ago. The owner had hoped to sell the location, so she had Lisa conduct an investigation and do a cleansing on the property. The

Early Shawnee teems with life and modern electricity. *Courtesy of the Pottawatomie County Museum.*

owner at that time claimed a young man had committed suicide in one of the upstairs rooms—he possibly died of an overdose. Lisa was kind enough to share her stories of what they encountered when they investigated the building. She reported that getting into the building was a little tricky since most of the main entryways had been boarded up. The owner had to explain how to gain entry with some careful maneuvering. The building was in a sorry state, with trash and old stained mattresses scattered around the floor. It soon became apparent that this was a homeless man's refuge from some of the colder nights.

There was no electricity in the building, so the team had to rely on their flashlights to help guide them through a maze of broken glass and fallen bricks. They yelled out to announce their arrival, in case there were any living bodies hiding out among the broken walls of the building. Once they ascended the set of rickety old stairs, they reached the second level of the building, where the walls were lined with small rooms, and they all had a number to help identify one room from the next. The rooms were small, with only enough space for one small bed and a small dresser. One common restroom was located, which would have been shared at the time, but at the time, it laid in waste, as vandals had made quick work to destroy it. The team witnessed various things throughout the evening, including objects that seemed to fall from the ceilings and walls, but they were never able to locate the source or the objects that had fallen.

The team focused their investigation on the floor with an EVP session. On reviewing their audio equipment, they discovered some voices. One was of a young man who seemed to be very sad; the other appeared to be a woman's voice. When asked what her name was, the voice replied, "I've been here so long, I can't remember my name." The woman appeared very distraught. Another EVP of her was heard asking for help. Lisa and her team concluded their investigation with a cleansing of the building; they burned sage and offered up prayers to help the spirits pass on and find peace in the afterlife. The team has not been back to the location since. The owner had hoped to sell the location, looking for someone who might do something with it, but to this day, the building remains boarded up and in disrepair. Sitting just outside the building is a monument that contains the town's time capsule, which is to be opened on May 7, 2104. Perhaps by then, the building will have taken on a new chapter, revitalizing its long history from the heyday of the Santa Fe Railroad.

22
Personal Relics
Green's Corner Antiques

Located a little farther east of the railroad tracks, on Main Street, there is a little antique shop on the southwest corner of the road. But don't let its size fool you; this shop is anything but little. Once visitors step through its doors, they soon realize just how expansive the place really is.

Before Tanya stepped foot into the shop, she found herself drawn to it. She even circled the block three times before stopping to park and look back at the building. Her interest was piqued, and she knew she was picking up on something coming from the building, but she wasn't quite sure what. Tanya was first met by the cutest little door greeter, a short, curly-haired dog that loved to be petted. She looked around the shop a bit, trying to see what she could feel, and it didn't take long before the feelings came rushing in. Tanya was drawn to one particular area in the far southwest corner of the store. After her turn about the building, she decided to approach the owner to see what further information she could give.

Shawna, one of the shop's owners, was very helpful in answering some of the questions Tanya had. It is always hard to open a line of communication with someone you've never met when your line of questioning concerns a ghost. Tanya handed the owner her card and started off by saying what she would normally say: "So, this is going to sound strange, but I was wondering if you have any ghost stories or haunted history that you would like to share?" To Tanya's surprise, Shawna proved to be a fountain of knowledge and stories, and she was more than happy to share her experiences.

Antique shops not only carry a vast array of treasures from the past, they can also hold objects that retain a spirit or two. Paranormal investigators refer to these items as haunted objects. Not all antiques have an attachment to them, but some occasionally do, and in the field of paranormal research, these items are sometimes encountered in clients' homes. A home may have one or two haunted objects from the resident's collection, but an antique shop is prone to have many more. Green's Corner proved to have a long history of ghostly encounters due to its collection of haunted antiques.

Green's Corner has functioned as an antique store in Shawnee for the past thirty years. Prior to that, it was known as the Santa Fe Market and Grocery and Meat from 1928 to 1932. From there, it became a cleaner and hatter's store and a lumber store. Several storefronts are occupied by the building today, which once housed a cobbler shop and barbershop. Shawna and her family purchased the location a few years before I met her. Today, all the storefronts connect to form one large antique store, with several rooms going off in various directions. The floor plan is a labyrinth, leaving visitors to wonder if the rooms ever end.

Shawna said they started noticing strange things occurring the moment they purchased the building. Each night, she would go through the store to turn off lights, leaving the center ones near the front register for last. She would pull each light's string to turn them off one at a time as she went. After making her rounds, she would return to the front of the store to find objects placed neatly in the middle of the aisle floor—objects that she knew had not been there before, since she had just passed that way. A spirit that dwelled in the shop often made herself known by becoming a little more physical. She would often hit women's purses whenever they would walk near or through her area of the store. Cold spots are often felt in the store, and at times, knocking can be heard in various areas of the building.

Other things have been witnessed over the years as well. Once, a mother and son were alone in the shop, looking over items, when they came to the front to ask if anyone else was there. When they were told that they were the only customers there at that time, they became visibly upset. They stated that they had just heard someone talking to them in the back rooms. Then, the lights started flickering on and off. The shopper became so distressed that she made her husband join her for the duration of her shopping tour.

One spirit that used to haunt an area in the building was that of a man who often seemed sad. After the man had passed away, the shop had purchased several of his personal items from his estate sale to place in the store. Near the space where his items sat, the air sometimes seemed heavy and gloomy. He had collected Judy Garland items, so whenever he seemed to be sad, Shawna would play him one of the Judy Garland records. The atmosphere would instantly change. Another haunted object that Shawna said she had encountered was an old replica wooden refrigerator, a simple child's toy. It was purchased in a lot from another estate sale. The woman had passed away, and her daughter had inherited a large quantity of her belongings. The daughter felt her mother's spirit may have been attached to one of the objects, and she was right. It just happened to be attached to the most unlikely object in the collection.

Another spirit that was also well known at the store was that of an angry man. He would wander around the store, but no one knew who he was or if he was attached to the store or an object there. Some have witnessed a dark shadow in the form of a person in various locations around the shop, but the angry spirit has not been seen or felt in a while, so it is possible that he left the area attached to an object that had once been held at the store.

Shawna claimed she had never seen a ghostly apparition prior to obtaining the store, but she did believe in their existence. She received her own personal message from the other side after she lost a dear friend to cancer. Never witnessing anything supernatural up to that time, she told her friend that if she was going to try to get her attention, she needed to do something big to get it. Her friend did not disappoint. Shawna was sitting up at the front of the store when she started hearing a beeping sound, like an alarm going off, coming from the front window area. She looked for something that could have possibly been making the sound. She finally located an old clock radio box among her friend's things that she had brought up to the store. Shawna had left the box behind the counter, never opening it, figuring she would get to it later. She wondered how the old clock could have possibly been making sounds and how the batteries could have lasted so long, but she didn't think much more about it and soon forgot all about it. It wasn't until later, when she noticed the box was sitting behind the register, that she decided to pick it up and see what it was that had been making the alarm sound. Once Shawna opened the box, she was shocked to find that the alarm clock listed on the front of the box was not what was in the box at all. Instead, the box held nothing but a collection of old rubber fishing worms—nothing that could have been making that noise or any other noise. It was then that she realized her friend had done something to get her attention. She had drawn her attention to a box that contained objects from something they had often shared as a favorite pastime: fishing. Shawna knew she had received a message from her friend. She asked her to do something big, and in her eyes, she did, and her message was received.

At the end of their talk, Tanya told Shawna the area she felt the most energy in was the far southwest corner of the store. Shawna said that seems to be where most people pick up on the energy. At one point, that area had served as a one-room home, where the owners of one of the shops used to live. It is no wonder the energy seems to linger on there. Shawna stated that the store seems to be a little less active these days, as far as the spirits are concerned. Some seem to have moved on with purchased items, but Shawna does believe they get the random transient ghost from time to time. That being said, new (or old) items are being added to the store's inventory frequently, so no one can tell what spirit will show up next.

23
Lingering Impressions
Twenty West Main

Near the corner of Main and Beard Streets, there is a four-story, red brick building that has stood there since the late 1800s. From a unique boutique to a medical marijuana dispensary, this building has been home to many small businesses in Shawnee. One of the more well-known businesses was the J.L. Roebuck Co. and Hardware, which dealt in implements for wagons and buggies. The old painted sign that was located on the east-facing wall can still be seen lining one of the interior walls of the building. This once-exterior wall has since been closed in by the addition of extra floors that are connected to the building directly to its east. It is believed that one of the building's male spirits may have originated from this time.

When the current owners bought the building, they weren't aware that it came with some resident spirits. The first accounts of paranormal activity occurred when one of the tenants was in the back area, near the stairs. While there, she happened to glance up and see a man in a white shirt going up the stairs. She thought it seemed a little funny to see a man there, especially one in clothing that didn't quite fit in with today's fashion. When she looked back, she found that he had quickly disappeared. Left a little unnerved and shaken, the woman approached the owner and reported what she had just witnessed; she described the man in detail, including the look of his white shirt. The owner showed her some old photographs of the interior of the building; some contained images of men in them. The woman was surprised to see that the man she had just witnessed going up the stairs was one of the men in the photograph that had been taken almost a century ago.

How the 200 block of Main Street appeared a century ago. *Courtesy of the Pottawatomie County Museum.*

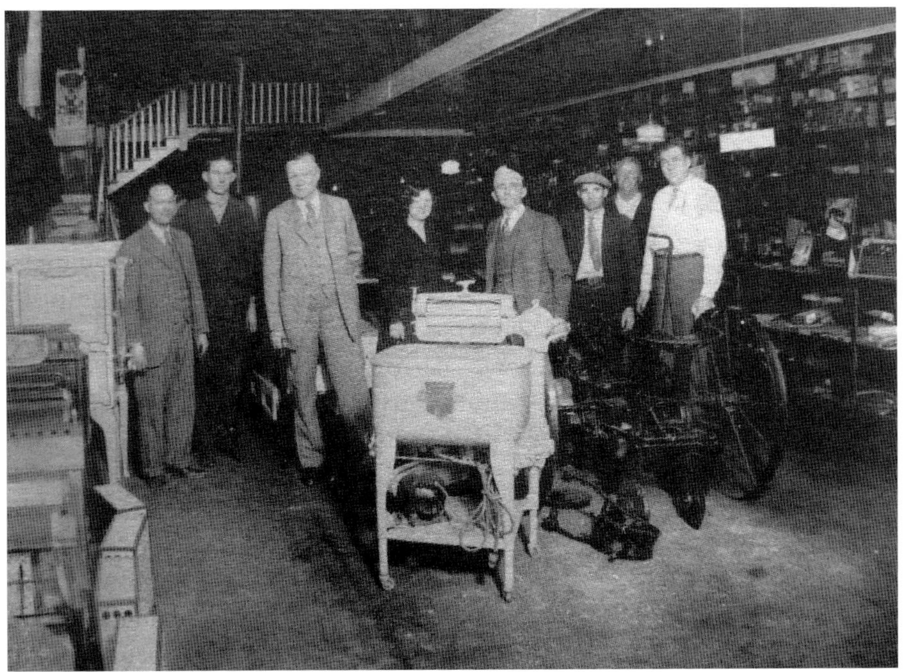

The phantom man on the stairs was recognized in this old photograph. *McCoy photograph.*

The owners, as well as other tenants, continued to witness more and more instances of paranormal activity. Renovations are currently underway on the upper floors, which sit empty, aside from various work tools and some old pieces of furniture and fixtures. As Tanya was interviewing the owner about their experiences, she was gracious enough to show me around the building and share the locations and stories of all the paranormal activities that the occupants have witnessed. Tanya asked her if she would mind her bringing in her team of paranormal investigators to see if they could contact any of the spirits that may reside in her building. She agreed, and the date was set.

The team arrived on a cold February night. It had been steadily drizzling throughout the day, which only helped to intensify the eerie feeling of the deserted downtown area. As they entered the building, they were shown down a long hallway to the back of the shops, which opened into a large sitting area. Comfy chairs, tables and rugs were scattered around the room, giving it a warm, inviting feeling. They started to set up their equipment, checking batteries and preparing for the night. Before they even completed the equipment check, the instruments all started reacting. Lights and sounds were emanating from all the various equipment. The team scanned the room with the equipment, trying to locate a possible cause for the sudden energy flux, but they were unable to locate the source. They soon realized that the energy fields were actively moving around the room, causing shifts in cold spots and spikes on their EMF detectors. High readings were obtained from inanimate objects, such as one round table in the middle of the room. The readings were not found under the table or above the table, where they would normally have been picked up if there had been a wiring issue. There was no rhyme or reason as to why the team's equipment would be acting in this way. They concluded that it must be paranormal.

Once the team left the common area, they ascended the stairs to the third floor to start their investigations. Throughout the ascent, their equipment continued to react to an unseen energy source. Many of them had ghost radios going at this time, and words began flooding in. One of the entities that started to come through seemed to be—or at least seemed to present itself as—a young child. They encountered this spirit a few more times throughout the investigation. Many people in the group, especially the females, reported feeling an unwelcomed emotion on the second floor. The group agreed that what many of them felt was the presence of a male entity who did not like females on his floor. As the team's equipment continued to react, their ghost radios began to identify two men by name. One name

Left: The façade of 20 East Main Street today. *McCoy photograph.*

Right: The stairs where the man appeared decades after his death. *McCoy photograph.*

was Jake; the other was Robert or Rob. Both names came up several times throughout the investigation and on multiple people's devices.

The group explored the third and fourth floors. Even though some activity was witnessed on all the floors, the most active floor that night was the second floor. The team decided to return to that floor to see what further evidence they could obtain there. As they sat around the open area of the second floor, many people started to experience a negative feeling. In one room, the movement of a shadow figure could be seen darting from one side of the doorway to the next. One investigator even felt as if someone was touching her neck. The moment she mentioned it, one of the ghost radios said the word "neck."

As the night progressed, the activity took a more sinister turn. Negative words started to come across the ghost radio, and the atmosphere in the room began to feel heavy. The room seemed to be enshrouded by a whole new darkness. Many people began feeling an uneasy emotion coming over them. With the activity starting to turn negative, Tanya was asked to conduct a cleansing prayer in the hope of calming the negative activity.

How 20 East Main Street appeared in the boomtown days of Shawnee. *McCoy photograph.*

Prayers were done throughout the second floor of the building, and as Tanya dismissed her team, she stayed behind to do a special prayer with the owner in the hope of calming the atmosphere for everyone who had to remain in the building.

On conclusion of the investigation, the team and Tanya felt that there were two prominent male spirits in the building, and there were possibly more. The two male spirits, whom the investigators now refer to as Jake and Robert, appear to occupy the upper floors and claim them as their own with a strict "no women allowed" policy. Perhaps in time, the two spirits will be able to catch up with the modern age, which is no longer just a man's world, and learn to coexist in the old historic building they seem to call home.

24
A Stroll Down Main Street
More Stories of Downtown Shops

Shawnee's downtown practically buzzes with the energy of the past. As the first major stop on the railroad as it headed out of Indian Territory and into the wilds of the Oklahoma Territory, it swarmed with travelers who were looking for a good time. Saloons along the south side of town were packed with legal drinkers. It is said that, at some time or another, just about every establishment downtown had a brothel upstairs—or at least a boardinghouse where owners looked the other way. Even after the day statewide prohibition came in 1907, downtown remained busy, as generations of shops had keepers and customers who still seemed to visit.

Past to Present Marketplace

7 West Main Street

The enthusiastic personality of Shawnee is evident in its architecture, especially in the building that hosts Past to Present, where curious visitors can still see the rooms where it all happened. One of the current owners said that it was once Shawnee's premier brothel. Through the years, as tamer times settled in the town, the building was home to Gibson's Department Store. It was a radical change for the building, as the upstairs area became the children's section, filled with toys. After Gibson's, the building hosted swap meets and, finally, a store for antiques. Today, the upstairs area retains

Above: Nothing but the finest in women's apparel for Shawnee residents. *Courtesy of the Pottawatomie County Museum.*

Left: A man-shaped watermark above the door at Past and Present is said to be a shadow of a past resident. *Provine photograph.*

its layout as a long common room with numerous bedrooms off to the west side. The original wallpaper, which is over a century old, still hangs, hinting at the decadence of the institution. Today, it is used for storage, except one room, which is kept empty, since putting things there seems to rile up one of the three different spirits said to haunt the building.

One spirit is the phantom of a lady dressed in white. Time and again, people claim to see her upstairs, just out of the corners of their eyes. As they turn to get a better look, they find themselves alone. Another spirit is the shadow of a man who appears in the window. Several people have claimed to see him peeking out at the street, which is quite a trick since the window has been blocked off for years. The third spirit ventures downstairs, moving items on shelves and even calling out to the living. Once, while one of the owners was leaving out the back after locking up, a voice called out, "Are you going?" She stopped and asked, "Who is that?" There was no reply, and a thorough search of the store revealed no living soul. One owner remains skeptical, saying she has never seen or felt anyone there, despite being on the second floor for hours at a time. She noted, "If they are up there, they need to pay their rent. They're way behind!"

THE OWL SHOPPE

8 East Main Street

A little hometown diner known as the Owl Shoppe is opened only for lunch, Tuesday through Saturday, and for one evening meal on Friday night, but it has offered countless delicious meals to the residents of Shawnee for many years. Built in 1898, this building housed one of Shawnee's first hardware stores. Later, it became a jewelry shop and optician's office. In 1923, it housed a city pool hall, and with it being during the Roaring Twenties, one can only imagine what activities may have occurred there at the time. In the 1930s, the building was converted into a restaurant, and later, it became a barbershop, a music shop and then the Richard Bros. Owl Drugstore, which is what it remained for many years. The old drugstore, like most drugstores at the time, had an old soda shop counter. The machines that produced the shakes of malts that were enjoyed so often during that time can still be seen behind the counter today.

The long soda counter extends toward the back of the café. Red-topped, old-fashioned stools line the countertop, welcoming visitors to have a seat and order a quick, delicious meal. The waitstaff is friendly, and they give the diner a real hometown feel—like so many mom and pop diners offer. Various small tables scatter the open-spaced floor plan of the café. Along the east wall, shelves and drawers that appear to be original still stand, giving visitors a glimpse into what the original shop's displays must have looked like.

The ghostly activity that occurs in the building tends to be the common activity we often see in so many of these old historic buildings: noises and movement. The sounds of creaking floors, as if someone is walking by, and various bumps can often be heard around the room prior to guests arriving. From time to time, appliances will suddenly turn on by themselves, as if being operated by an unseen set of hands. Some report feeling an unsettling emotion when walking toward the back of the building to use the restroom. They say it makes them feel as if they are not quite alone. The staff continues their daily work cheerfully and free of worry about any of the spirits that may haunt the old building. They don't feel threatened by their presence; they happily coexist, greeting the daily customers as they come to enjoy lunch at the historic Owl Shoppe.

ASH, OAK AND THORN

112 East Main Street

Untold thousands of pairs of feet have crossed the threshold of 112 East Main Street, which served as numerous shoe stores throughout the early twentieth century, including Up-to-Date in 1923, Earnest Brothers in 1928 and Gann Shoe Company in 1937. According to the Pottawatomie County Historical Society, the building was opened as Frauenthal Bros. Furniture in 1901 and has hosted a few other enterprises through the years, such as Wright Jewelers and Barnett's Menswear. Today, the building is home to a shop for gifts, teas and curios. Its walls sparkle with jewelry, tapestries, prayer flags and candles. The door opens to loudly ringing bells, which its proprietor, Lorna, enjoys, since she can hear them anywhere in the back. "Besides," she adds, "the nastier things don't like bells, so that keeps them away."

She shared a story of an unseen visitor who stopped by the shop. Lorna was working late one night when her dog suddenly began to whimper and slink close before finally trying to crawl into her lap, despite being much too big. It felt as if someone was there in the shop with them. She called out, "If anyone's here—leave the dog alone! Don't bother anybody, and you can't come home with me." The dog relaxed, and the presence seemed to be content with that deal. Lorna noted that it isn't just her shop that has activity. With several of Shawnee's neighborhoods' origins dating back over a century, "Lots of people have old houses. Some of them want to get rid of negative energies." She said, "I sell a lot of salt and sage," which seems to do the trick just fine.

THE ARTS @317

317 East Main Street

In 1928, the building was home to the lively Bell Restaurant, and, later, the Shawnee Bowling Parlor. Through the years it's hosted furniture stores, the Shawnee Electric Company and even a poultry hatchery. Today, the Arts @317 uses the space to highlight Oklahoma talent in visual arts and sewing.

As the building was being transformed into a modern gallery and workspace, it was clear that something from the past lingered there. Workmen who came into the building in the morning noted that their tools had been moved around overnight. The doors had been locked, and anyone who had gotten inside would likely have made off with the valuable equipment; instead, they were simply placed elsewhere. Even while they were there, radios the workers had set up for entertainment would suddenly change stations, specifically to the oldies. One worker said that it even ejected a CD of healing chants and instead played rock 'n roll. Most famously, the workmen reported the sounds of kids laughing and playing in the back room. Even to this day, several people have heard them and gone to investigate, but they have never found any children there. Nothing there seems threatening, although dogs that visit the space will bristle every time they approach the ladies' room in the back. They refuse to go anywhere near it, despite being fine with the rest of the building.

The biggest clue that something paranormal was going on came after the staff had diligently hung art on the walls for the first children's art show. When they came in the next morning, every picture had been taken down and set along the base of the wall. It didn't appear as if they had fallen; they were in a different order and carefully propped up. Since nothing had been broken or even bent, they decided that whoever it was just had their own display in mind. They rehung the pictures in the new order and never had a problem with them again.

Few would think of such haunts in a charming shop. *Provine photograph.*

Even today, the lights will turn themselves on and off, and things will move around on the shelves overnight. Staff said that they had the building saged, after which the moving slowed down. They said they sometimes suggest out loud that they'll do it again, which seems to give a hint to the spirit behind the activity that it had flared up too much.

25

Invited In

2 East Main Street

Towering at the center of downtown Shawnee, the multi-story, brick-and-concrete building at 2 East Main Street is the embodiment of the town's history coming together with the present. The building, which was opened in 1927, started out as the home of the State National Bank. It was celebrating its twenty-fifth year in business and was flush with oil money. Just six years later, however, the Great Depression caught up with the Oklahoma oil fields. Sales fell, along with oil prices. Loans defaulted, and the bank closed on a moratorium in 1933, trading hands to be resurrected as American National Bank. Back in business, the bank continued in its tower until 1965, when it moved to the newly built home at the corner of Broadway and Ninth Streets. There, ANB was acquired by Arvest in 1998.

The old State National building gained a new life when the One Ten Broadcast Group moved in. The company was started in Seminole with a three-thousand-watt station. The broadcasts doubled their wattage to become KIRC, which is said to stand for "Keep It Real Country." Moving the studio to Shawnee created a backup and allowed the group to expand, with stations for oldies and AM talk stations. The move came along with a major remodel of the lobby, where booths and broadcasting equipment, along with modern offices, were installed to replace the high-ceilinged main floor of the bank. Whether they had been stirred up through the renovations or had arrived on their own, the spirits of the past are active in the tower.

Account manager Rita Sloan related that at least one of the spirits could very well be a banker who is said to have committed suicide in the

The old blends with the new as old bank signs hang alongside the new radio station. *Provine photograph.*

An expansive bank lobby made for classy business in early Shawnee. *Courtesy of the Pottawatomie County Museum.*

second-floor vault during the turbulent Great Depression. He is said to linger in the building, sometimes refiling documents and shifting things around in offices. One night soon after the station's move, Sloan said she became especially aware of a presence while covering the broadcast of a high school football game. She said she heard papers shuffling down the hall and was surprised that someone else was still in the building so late, so she went to check out the noise. Each of the offices was empty; yet, she could hear someone going through papers, as if they were moving them around the main floor, looking for something. Sloan began to get chills, as if someone was following her. She retreated back to the studio and locked the door. She said, "I knew that wasn't going to do much help since what's a door to a ghost? But at least I wouldn't hear it shuffling those papers!"

Now sealed up, these stairs were once part of the "Shawnee Tunnels." *Provine photograph.*

The basement is said to be especially spooky, despite the encouraging paintings on the walls of the main rooms that came from the time it hosted a dojo. It carries a sense of heaviness in the air, and people insist on feeling that someone is there with them, watching. Several visitors have claimed to smell cigarettes from an unseen smoker who then follows them until they head back upstairs.

Remodels through the years have created something of a twisting labyrinth, with rooms for storage, an old breakroom, an indoor well hidden among the utilities and a cement-covered stairway that is said to be part of the "Shawnee Tunnels." Rather than a systematic flow of passages, such as those of the Underground in Oklahoma City, Shawnee held several connected basements to enable people to go from one building to another without having to step outside. The "tunnel" there was said to run next door when it was a jewelry store, allowing jewelers to store their wares in the bank's vault without risking being jumped in the street. According to legends, many more of the buildings were connected at one time for the more illicit purposes of smuggling booze or allowing well-to-do folks who wanted to pay a visit to the unmentionable spots to sneak in.

Sloan said that some of the staff wouldn't even go down to the basement after an incident occurred with a paranormal investigator who wanted to research the space with his daughter. She said she had escorted them down to one of the smaller rooms that has an especially strong oppressive energy in it. The investigators set up a talking board printed with short phrases and letters of the alphabet. Placing their hands on the planchette, they prompted the spirit to reach out by moving it toward words. They asked, "If someone is here, would they like to talk?" The planchette moved toward "no." The investigators attempted to move it away for more questions, but the planchette slid back to "no" over and over again. When they released it, the wooden block began spinning faster and faster. Sloan said that was when she felt someone touch the hair on the back of her head. She spun to find no one there, so she ran out of the room, across the basement and completely up the stairs. Without going back down, she called to the investigators that they should wrap up their research. They had already begun packing up their things to hurry after her.

With its history of haunts, the current owners of One Ten generously offer the building up for ghost tours during the Boo on Bell celebrations around Halloween and for fundraisers for programs like Safe Events for Families. Armed with paranormal investigation equipment that measures fluxes in electromagnetic fields, records EVPs and interprets signals, tourists see what they can find when they reach across the veil in the basement as well as in the old offices in the upper floors. One guest had a story of when she was prompted to knock at a door. Thinking it was a gag with someone hiding on the other side, she declined, but the hosts insisted and even unlocked it to show an empty room beyond. They closed it, she knocked and something on the other side knocked back. Another story of the KIRC building comes from an older Boo on Bell event, the 13 Spirits of Shawnee Terror-tory Ghost Walk. Performed as a fundraiser for the Shawnee High School Drama Club in the mid-2000s, students dressed in costumes would present terrifying tales from the history of Shawnee. After one walk, a guest asked why they hadn't stopped to talk to the girl at the radio station. "We don't have a stop at the radio station," the guide told him. The guest shook his head. "I saw a girl in Depression-era clothes standing right next to the doors to the radio station. She was watching us, like she was waiting on us to come over." He pointed back to the overhang where he said she stood. The girl was gone, and no one else had seen her.

BIBLIOGRAPHY

Books

Butler, Ken. *Oklahoma Renegades: Their Deeds and Misdeeds*. Gretna, LA: Pelican Publishing Company, 1997.

Etter, Jim Marion. *Ghost-Town Tales of Oklahoma: Unforgettable Stories of Nearly Forgotten Places*. Stillwater, OK: New Forums Press, 1996.

Fortson, John. *Pott Country and What Has Come of It*. Shawnee, OK: Pottawatomie County Historical Society, 1936.

McDonald, Ann Lanier. *History of Disasters in Shawnee Oklahoma*. Scotts Valley, CA: CreateSpace, 2016.

Palmer, Barbara. *Oklahoma Off the Beaten Path*. Guilford, CT: Globe Pequot Press, 1996.

Documentary

Jacob, Steve. "Native American Paranormal Project Presents Grisso Mansion." www.youtube.com.

Articles

Alexander, M.J. "The Human Wolves of Konawa." *Slice*, October 2013.

Ast, Nicholas. "Gerrer, Gregory (1867–1946)." *Encyclopedia of Oklahoma History and Culture*, n.d.

B., Steve. "Pottawatomie County, OK Encounters." www.dogmanencounters.com.

Carter, Kathryn. "Ghosts of Tecumseh Past Whisper from Vacant Lot." *Countywide & Sun*, August 14, 2019.

Defrange, Ann, and Ann Weaver. "Cities Fought to Claim Capital." *Oklahoman*, November 16, 2006.

Encyclopedia Britannica. "Jim Thorpe." www.britannica.com.

———. "Seminole." www.britannica.com.

Fariss, David. "The Oklahoma Terror, aka Pretty Boy Floyd." *Edmond Life & Leisure*, December 14, 2017.

Farley, Tracy. "Vandals Vanquish 90-Year-Old Bridge." *Shawnee News-Star*, October 8, 1992.

Hoagland, Bruce W. "Cross Timbers." *Encyclopedia of Oklahoma History and Culture*, n.d.

Hofsommer, Donovan L. "Missouri-Kansas-Texas Railroad." Texas State Historical Association. Published June 15, 2010. www.tshaonline.org.

Horcher, Gary. "'Romulus & Remus.' Oklahoma's Strangely Named Towns." *Oklahoman*, April 17, 1999.

KOCO 5 News. "UFO Caught on Live TV Flying over Oklahoma City." www.koco.com.

Konawa Genealogical Society. "Konawa." *Encyclopedia of Oklahoma History and Culture*, n.d.

Kraft, Lisa A. "Citizen Potawatomi." *Encyclopedia of Oklahoma History and Culture*, n.d.

Kuhlman, Annette. "Kickapoo." *Encyclopedia of Oklahoma History and Culture*, n.d.

Mize, Jeff. "Earlsboro." *Encyclopedia of Oklahoma History and Culture*, n.d.

Mullins, William H. "Seminole County." *Encyclopedia of Oklahoma History and Culture*, n.d.

Musslewhite, Lynn, and Suzanne Jones Crawford. "Barnard, Catherine Ann." *Encyclopedia of Oklahoma History and Culture*, n.d.

National Register of Historic Places. "Barnard Elementary School." www.nps.org.

Perkins Yates, Roxann. "OKLAHOMA MYSTERIES: Her Tombstone Reads: 'Murdered by Human Wolves.'" *Red Dirt Report*, December 2, 2014.

Pottawatomie County Genealogy Club. "State National Bank, Shawnee, Pottawatomie Co., OK." www.sites.rootsweb.com.

Revolvy. "Governor's Mansion (Shawnee, Oklahoma)." www.revolvy.com.

Shawnee Daily Herald. "Murdered in a Lonely Pasture." May 12, 1909.

Shawnee Daily News. "Ghost Haunts This Pasture?" January 23, 1911.
———. "House Haunted? Low Rent!" April 2, 1911.
Shawnee Daily News-Herald. "Dastardly Crime Laid to Ed Berry." July 12, 1915.
Shawnee News. "Gorman Is Victim of Strange Circumstances." December 13, 1909.
———. "To Offer Reward for Mysterious Assailant." September 6, 1911.
Smith, Shane. "Infamous Konawa Gravestone Stolen. Again." *Red Dirt Report*, October 27, 2016.
Steffen, Bree. "Professors Solve Mystery of Flying Light across Oklahoma Sky." KOCO 5 News. www.koco.com.
Tecumseh Republican. "Anent the Indian Burning." January 21, 1898.
Trotter, Gloria. "Tecumseh Opera House in Need of Repairs." *Countywide & Sun*, March 19, 2018.
Tyler, Carl N. "Shawnee Trail." *Encyclopedia of Oklahoma History and Culture*, n.d.
Veenendaal, Augustus J., Jr. "Chicago, Rock Island and Pacific Railway." *Encyclopedia of Oklahoma History and Culture*, n.d.
Visit Shawnee. "The Aldridge: Jewel of Historic Downtown Shawnee." Published June 5, 2018. www.visitshawnee.com.
White, James D. "Sacred Heart Abbey." *Encyclopedia of Oklahoma History and Culture*, n.d.
Wilson, Linda D. "Sac and Fox Opening." *Encyclopedia of Oklahoma History and Culture*, n.d.
Wright, Catherine, and Mary Ann Anders. "Sacred Heart Mission Site." National Register of Historic Places. www.nps.org.

Websites

Cinema Treasures. "Ritz Theater." www.cinematreasures.org.
Citizen Potawatomi Nation. www.potawatomi.org.
City of Shawnee, Oklahoma. "Shawnee Forgotten Hub of Central Oklahoma." www.old.shawneeok.org.
Eastern Shawnee Tribe of Oklahoma. www.estoo-nsn.gov.
Find A Grave Memorial. "Sarah Elizabeth Godsey Cross (1836–1915)." www.findagrave.com.
First Nations Histories. "Kickapoo." www.tolatsga.org.
Ghosts of America. "Shawnee, Oklahoma, Ghost Sightings." www.ghostsofamerica.com.
Mount Saint Mary's. "Our History." www.mountstmary.org.

Ohio History Central. "Shawnee Indians." www.ohiohistorycentral.org.
Sac and Fox Nation of Missouri. "History of the Tribe." www.sacandfoxks.com.
———. "Welcome to the Sac and Fox Nation." www.sacandfoxnation-nsn.gov.
Shadowlands. "Shadowlands Haunted Places Index—Oklahoma." www.theshadowlands.net.
Shawnee Tribe. www.shawnee-tribe.com.
St. Gregory's Abbey. "Our History." www.monksok.org.
Waymarking. "The Bison Theater—Shawnee, OK—Vintage Movie Theaters on Waymarking.com." www.waymarking.com.
———. "Governor's Mansion—Shawnee, OK—U.S. National Register of Historic Places on Waymarking.com." www.waymarking.com.
Wilkerson, April. "About Us." Jones Theatres. www.jonestheatres.com.
Wurtz, Maureen. "Haunted Oklahoma: Ritz Theater in Shawnee." ABC, KTUL 8. www.ktul.com.

About the Authors

Tanya McCoy

Tanya McCoy started researching the paranormal over two decades ago and has been actively investigating in the field since 2010. She is the founder of the Oklahoma Paranormal Association and a board member of the Mustang Oklahoma Historical Society. She has obtained an online degree in paranormal psychology and is currently teaching a paranormal research class and paranormal research versus quantum physics class at Francis Tuttle Technology Center in Oklahoma City. Born in California, she now calls the state of Oklahoma her home. She is a published children's book author and has been a nurse for over two decades. She has been seen on several television shows, including *My Ghost Story* (Syfy Channel), *Haunted Hospitals* (Travel Channel) and *Paranormal 911* (the Travel Channel), and she has also been featured in various news articles and has been seen on local news stations. She team-produces one of Oklahoma's annual paranormal conferences, which is usually centered on the Oklahoma City area, as well as special events throughout the year to help teach and train future paranormal investigators. In January 2020, she opened a metaphysical shop in downtown historic El Reno in the historic Rock Island Railroad offices, and she hopes to open Oklahoma's first paranormal museum, filled with haunted objects, bigfoot artifacts and articles that share the history and stories of ghosts, bigfoot, UFOs and other various cryptids found around the world. She currently conducts the downtown El Reno ghost walk, sharing the history of the town as well as its ghostly tales. She is working on several more books that focus on the paranormal, metaphysical and historical, and she is working on a book for her paranormal class. She is also working on her first fiction novel, which she hopes to print by 2021.

Jeff Provine

Raised on his family's Land Run farm, north of Enid, Jeff began collecting Oklahoma folklore in 2009, when he started a ghost tour at the University of Oklahoma. He has since added tours in downtown Norman and Oklahoma City. His other works include the "This Day in Alternate History" blog; "The Academy" webcomic; *31 Ghost Stories*, an illustrated series of urban legends; and *Okie Comics Magazine*. Jeff serves as professor of English at Oklahoma City Community College and lectures in creative writing and the history of comic books around the metropolitan area.